GOVERNMENT OFFICE
FOR LONDON

Strategic Guidance for London Planning Authorities

LONDON

RPG3 May 1996

London: HMSO

Published by HMSO and available from:

HMSO Publications Centre
(Mail, fax and telephone orders only)
PO Box 276, London SW8 5DT
Telephone orders 0171 873 9090
General enquiries 0171 873 0011
(queuing system in operation for both numbers)
Fax orders 0171 873 8200

HMSO Bookshops
49 High Holborn, London WC1V 6HB
(counter service only)
0171 873 0011 Fax 0171 831 1326
68-69 Bull Street, Birmingham B4 6AD
0121 236 9696 Fax 0121 236 9699
33 Wine Street, Bristol BS1 2BQ
0117 9264306 Fax 0117 9294515
9-21 Princess Street, Manchester M60 8AS
0161 834 7201 Fax 0161 833 0634
16 Arthur Street, Belfast BT1 4GD
01232 238451 Fax 01232 235401
71 Lothian Road, Edinburgh EH3 9AZ
0131 228 4181 Fax 0131 229 2734
The HMSO Oriel Bookshop
The Friary, Cardiff CF1 4AA
01222 395548 Fax 01222 384347

HMSO's Accredited Agents
(see Yellow Pages)

and through good booksellers

Note: Maps and diagrams in this document are indicative only.

If further information is required the relevant source given should be contacted.

Picture credits:

Chris Westwood – Environment Picture Library

Patrick Doherty – Image Bank

Metropolitan Police Service

COI

Crown Copyright – DoE – Brian Russel

London Tourist Board

Produced by DDP Services.

Cover design by COI.

Printed in Great Britain on recycled paper.

B3980. May 1996.

Contents

Foreword by
Rt Hon John Gummer MP,
Minister with Special Responsibility
for London, Chairman of the
Joint London Advisory Panel

London is one of the world's great cities. It has a vital place in the economic and cultural life of the United Kingdom. The whole nation has an interest in our capital maintaining and enhancing its status as a world city.

To do this London must become an even more attractive place to live, work and visit. Its citizens should be able to look forward to a good quality of life and a wide range of opportunities. London must adapt to survive, whilst preserving that which already makes it special.

The responsibility for London's future rests with Government, the Boroughs, business, other agencies, the voluntary sector and Londoners themselves. Only by bringing together all these interests, working in partnership, can we meet the challenge. All have been involved in the widespread consultation process leading to the production of this Strategic Guidance for London Planning Authorities, and I hope that all will have regard to it as it impacts on their interests and responsibilities.

The Guidance is not, and should not be, a prescriptive document. It is not a detailed plan for London: that would impinge upon the local decision-making process, which is quite properly the responsibility of local planning authorities, in the light of local knowledge and circumstances. But the Government has a duty to set clear policies and a strategic framework to guide those authorities in preparing their Unitary Development Plans and in exercising their development control responsibilities, taking account of national, regional, and London-wide priorities.

National guidance sets down the broad framework of Government planning policies. This Guidance interprets those policies as they apply to the special, often unique, circumstances of London. It must be read too in conjunction with the regional guidance for the South East of England and the Thames Gateway Planning Framework, for London does not function as an isolated entity. There is a complex and important inter-relationship between London and the surrounding counties on a wide range of matters from housing provision and employment through to transport and waste disposal. There can be no strategic planning for London which does not reach out beyond its traditional boundaries.

Sustainable development is the key to creating a better London in the twenty-first century, and it is a foundation upon which this Guidance is based. We must ensure that London remains an internationally competitive city, generating wealth and jobs, whilst at the same time enhancing the quality of life and reducing the city's impact on the environment. We must recognise that these goals are not alternatives, but complementary.

Maintaining a healthy economy for London means providing opportunities for the growth of new modern businesses and supporting those that already exist. We must build on London's world class strengths in sectors such as finance and business services, telecommunications and the media, the arts, culture and tourism. We must harness the expertise which exists in London's higher educational institutions and the financial power of the City to help maintain London's manufacturing base. The Manufacturing Initiative and the work of

London First are vital ingredients in this. But we must ensure that London has the sites, the facilities and the quality of environment that will be needed to attract the industries of the future.

Tourism will continue to play an important role in London's economy, and offers significant opportunities for growth. In the central and surrounding areas especially, local authorities should encourage the development of good quality new facilities, bearing in mind the identified shortage of hotel bed spaces to accommodate and attract visitors.

Regeneration opportunities exist in many areas of London, with the potential for creating new employment and revitalising local communities. The Guidance identifies some of the main areas of opportunity and encourages local partnerships to work together to draw up policies for their future. It sets out a locational framework for development which emphasises the opportunities in the Thames Gateway, the Lee Valley, the major sites on the edge of the Central Area, and parts of West and South West London facing structural change. It emphasises the importance of the new and improved transport infrastructure in many of these areas as a focus for new development. For example, the decision to develop Stratford as a pivotal point for the new Channel Tunnel Rail Link will be a major boost to the regeneration of this part of London.

A new strategic vision is needed too for the Thames. We must restore the river, which ought to be one of London's greatest assets, to its proper place at the heart of the capital. It should become a focus for London life, not a physical and psychological dividing line. Separate guidance is being prepared for the Thames to help achieve this.

A sustainable future means improving the quality of London's natural and built environment. London's heritage of outstanding buildings, parks and open spaces reflect a confident and glorious past. This must be protected and preserved, and we should be adding to it and enhancing it. London's hosting of the millennium celebrations should provide an exciting opportunity for new projects and facilities that will be our bequest to future generations. These should reflect London's international status and confirm the confidence which we have in its future.

London needs to develop more sustainable patterns of transport in order to safeguard its status as a world city and an attractive place to live. The Government is publishing separately a transport strategy for London. This Guidance indicates how the planning system can help to secure an efficient transport system for London. Local authorities, transport providers and operators should seek to coordinate land use planning with decisions on transport provision to reduce the need to travel, especially by car, and to promote public transport, walking and cycling.

A sustainable future means not only protecting the historic heart of London, but also the town centres and urban villages which are the focus of local communities and activities in the suburbs. The Guidance stresses the importance of developing strategies for safeguarding the health and vitality of these centres, for encouraging more mixed use, and for ensuring easy access to shops, services and facilities for everyone.

We must use all available mechanisms to provide Londoners with a better quality of life. A holistic approach towards London's future must address a wide range of issues - employment and regeneration, education and competitiveness, transportation and the environment - and the inter-relationship between them. Delivering this complex agenda will not be easy, and it is vital that all the partners in London play their part. The new Joint London Advisory Panel, set up to advise the Government on strategic issues facing London, provides a forum for collaboration between the Government and the London Pride partners in tackling issues of common interest and in the development of a new shared vision for London. It reflects the recognition that we all have a role to play in ensuring that London remains a city of which Londoners and the country as a whole can be justly proud as we go forward into the new millennium.

Map 1 London and the South East Region

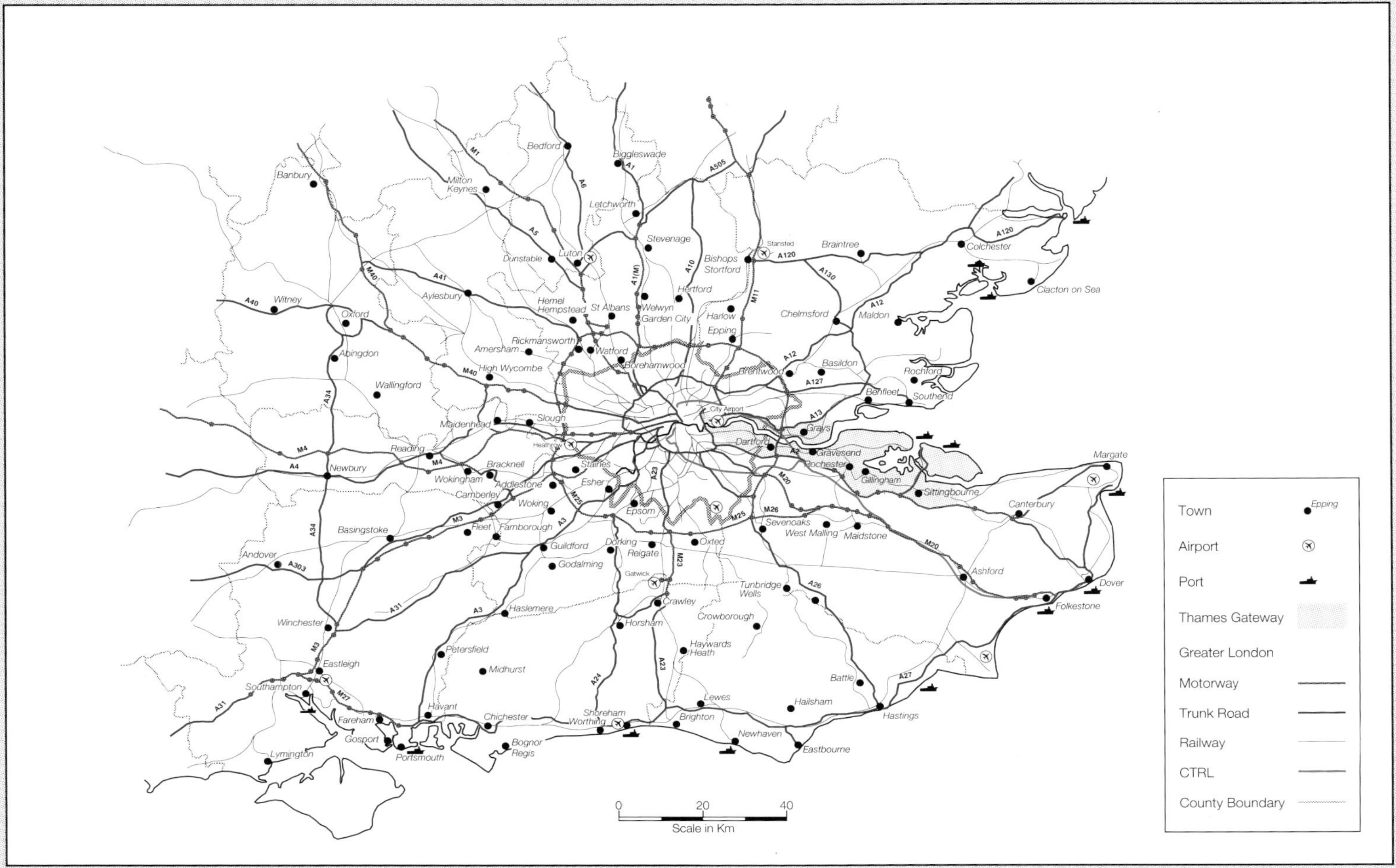

1. Introduction and Objectives

INTRODUCTION TO 1996 STRATEGIC PLANNING GUIDANCE

1.1.   London is a large and complex city at the heart of a dynamic region. It is the capital of the nation and one of the three financial capitals of the world. In terms of area it exceeds any other European city. In terms of population and output, it exceeds many European countries. It is a friendly, historic and beautiful city which attracts visitors from around the globe. It sits at the hub of national and international transport networks. It is a cosmopolitan and nuclear city, but has managed to preserve a strong sense of local community.

1.2.   London has the strengths and weaknesses of any city. The concentration of population creates the workforce and the market which make cities an attractive place to do business and supports a range of cultural and recreational activities that smaller communities could not sustain. However, the same concentration of population can create problems of congestion and pollution and can give rise to tensions. Like other cities, London must find ways of building on its strengths and tackling its weaknesses, because it must earn its living in an increasingly competitive environment. London must also adapt to change, as old industries decline and new emerge, and enthusiastically take up the challenge of sustainable development.

1.3.   The responsibility for London's future rests with business, with Government, with the Boroughs, with the voluntary sector and with Londoners. Although the Government is not the sole custodian of London's future, it does have a key part to play. In particular, it has a duty to give guidance to the Boroughs on the discharge of their planning responsibilities. (The term "Borough" throughout this Guidance refers to the 32 London Boroughs and the Corporation of the City of London).

1.4.   This Guidance is published by the Government Office for London (GOL), on behalf of the Secretary of State for the Environment (hereafter referred to as the Secretary of State). It has been prepared by the Government Office for London under the aegis of the Cabinet Sub-Committee for London and is endorsed by the Secretaries of State and Ministers of the Departments concerned with development in the capital.

1.5.   This Guidance has two main purposes. Its principal purpose is to give London Planning Authorities formal guidance from the Secretary of State for the Environment on the review of their Unitary Development Plans (UDPs). The UDPs specify what types of development will be permitted or encouraged in different areas of a Borough. The UDP carries great weight in the determination of individual planning applications. In influencing land use within the Borough, it can also have an impact on the local economy, the pattern of transport and the quality of life. A good UDP can attract business and direct it towards appropriate areas. It is important that businesses, voluntary organisations and individuals participate in the process of framing the UDP and understand the difficult balance which Boroughs have to strike.

1.6.   This document also sets land use planning issues in a broader context. It identifies important developments which Boroughs will wish to take into account in framing their UDPs. It highlights ways in which UDPs can contribute to promoting competitiveness and regeneration, stimulating economic activity and protecting the environment. It also sets out the strategic context within which all players involved in the future development of London and its buildings, activities, environment and transport systems should make their own decisions, by identifying the approach to development which the Government hopes to see taking place.

The regional context

1.7.   London must be seen in the context of the wider South East Region in which it is set, (Map 1). London has a complex relationship with the surrounding local authorities on matters such as housing provision, economic development, labour markets and transport systems. Boroughs on the edge of London will need to consider the relationship of their policies with those of neighbouring authorities. Central London includes many of the main capital and world city functions. Central Boroughs should have particular regard to the guidance for this area given in Chapter 2.

1.8.   This revised Strategic Planning Guidance has been prepared within the context of *Regional Planning Guidance for the South East* (RPG9). The Secretary of State issued RPG9 in March 1994. This sets out three key objectives for the region:

- enhanced economic performance

- sustainable development and environmental improvement

- opportunity and choice.

Further details will be found at paragraphs 1.7 - 1.9 of RPG9. Boroughs need to have regard to the interrelationships between London and the rest of the South East and the aim of regional guidance to reduce development pressure to the west of London and enhance growth in the east. The London Planning Advisory Committee (LPAC) and the South East Regional Planning Conference (SERPLAN) should ensure that strategic and regional issues are brought to the attention of their member authorities.

1.9.   *The Thames Gateway Planning Framework* was published in June 1995 (RPG9a). It establishes a set of principles to guide future development and environmental enhancement for the corridor stretching eastward from Deptford and Stratford. Supplementary Strategic Guidance for the River Thames is also in preparation. Riparian Boroughs should pay particular attention to the guidance contained in these documents as appropriate to their location. These documents and the Annex to RPG3 on Strategic Views published in November 1991 should be read with this strategic guidance as the Secretary of State's Guidance for London.

Structure of this Guidance

1.10.   This chapter sets out the objectives which underlie the Government's strategic framework for London. Chapter 2 describes the key locational components of London's structure which Boroughs should incorporate into their UDPs and which provide the framework for partnership activity to regenerate London's key corridors. The subsequent chapters give guidance on topics that should be included in UDPs. The Secretary of State asks that each Borough has particular regard to the points identified and considers them in reviews of UDPs. However, the general policy set out in these chapters should be used to inform decisions by all participants in the planning process.

1.11.   The Secretary of State is grateful for the advice which LPAC has offered in 1994 *Advice on Strategic Planning Guidance for London* (LPAC 1994a) which has had a significant impact on both the form and content of this Guidance. He looks to LPAC to further the objectives of this Guidance by assisting Boroughs in taking a strategic view on development issues and by keeping strategic issues under review so that the Guidance itself can be reviewed and kept up to date. He commends LPAC's "Four Fold Vision", which forms the basis of their advice (Fig 1.1).

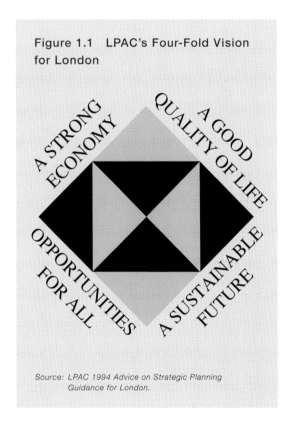

Figure 1.1   LPAC's Four-Fold Vision for London

A STRONG ECONOMY

A GOOD QUALITY OF LIFE

OPPORTUNITIES FOR ALL

A SUSTAINABLE FUTURE

Source: LPAC 1994 Advice on Strategic Planning Guidance for London.

1.12.   London contains diverse communities for which individual Boroughs are best placed to provide detailed policy. This Guidance does not attempt to deal with the many matters that are essentially local and which are best addressed by each local planning authority in preparing its UDP and in exercising its development control responsibilities.

1.13.   Many issues are not confined to one Borough, and many decisions have implications for neighbouring Boroughs and for London as a whole. The Secretary of State therefore expects local authorities to demonstrate that they have taken the wider issues into account and have coordinated their approach with neighbouring authorities. This will require more attention being given to Part I of UDPs, which cover strategic issues, together with appropriate reasoned justification. LPAC has an important role in monitoring and in advising on cross Borough issues, and the Secretary of State requests that they keep under review strategic planning matters, as noted in Chapter 10.

Objectives

1.14. The Government's objectives which are particularly relevant to this document are to:

- promote London as a world city, recognising its role as a world class business, commercial, educational and heritage centre

- maintain and enhance the competitiveness of business, including encouraging manufacturing, services, tourism, culture and the arts

- encourage a pattern of land use and provision of transport which minimises harm to the environment and reduces the need to travel especially by car, consistent with the principles of sustainable development

- promote urban regeneration, particularly in areas requiring physical improvement or the enhancement of employment opportunities, within the objectives for the South East Region as a whole

- enhance the vitality, viability and character of town and other local centres as shopping and community facilities that are accessible to all

- maximise housing provision in London, consistent with maintaining environmental quality, to meet the changing needs of the population

- maintain and improve the natural and open environment, including the Green Belt, Metropolitan Open Land and areas of national and international significance including the River Thames

- improve the quality and attractiveness of London's urban environment to benefit those who visit, live, work and do business in London

- facilitate the development of transport systems which are safe and efficient, and which contribute to the achievement of competitiveness, regeneration and environmental quality

- seek to improve air quality, to reduce waste, pollution and the use of energy, and to encourage recycling.

London: a world class city

1.15. London contributes around 15% of the UK's Gross Domestic Product, putting its economy on a par with large nation states. It occupies a unique position in the UK, Europe and the world.

1.16. London is also home to nearly 7 million people from diverse ethnic and cultural backgrounds. It has a labour pool of about 3.5 million people, many of whom are highly skilled and qualified. As a result of its extensive regional transport system, London employers have access to the largest regional labour pool in Europe - 9 million employees in the South East of England. As one of the world's top three financial centres and the world's largest centre for international bank lending, London contributes 75% of the UK's income from financial services. The financial and business services sector employs about 735,000 people, nearly 60% of whom work in the Central Area. London also retains an important manufacturing sector, employing nearly 330,000 people. London is home to 13 universities and 13 colleges of higher education. The Central Area is an important critical mass of business activity, enhanced by the wide variety of choice of offices in good locations supplemented by other concentrations, particularly in Docklands and Croydon.

1.17. The mix of a vibrant and diverse economy, a unique cultural heritage and quality of life, the vitality of its communities, and major strengths in communications, finance, and internal and international transport links have all helped London achieve its position as a world class city. With Heathrow, the world's busiest international airport, and the City Airport within its boundaries, with Gatwick and Stansted easily accessible by rapid links and with a new international rail terminal at Waterloo, London has excellent accessibility for international and european travellers. This combination of assets has led european businessmen to vote London as their most favoured location.

1.18. Boroughs should have regard to London's capital and world city status and make provision in their plans for enhancing and supporting this role. Many of the main capital and world city functions are concentrated in the Central Area, and central

Boroughs should have particular regard to the guidance for this area given in Chapter 2.

London: a city of change

1.19. Like all major cities London faces considerable challenges. Physical and economic structures have to change as the city adapts to new demands and new opportunities. International business has become increasingly mobile and is able to choose between different locations. Within Europe, rival cities such as Paris, Frankfurt, Barcelona and Berlin are competing more than ever to attract investment, business and jobs. Continuing developments in communications are likely to lead to even more competition in the future.

1.20. London's population has declined from its peak in 1939 of just over 8 million to under 7 million now. In inner London, the decline has been even more marked, from 5 million in the 1930s to under 3 million now. However, the years since 1984 have experienced a small increase in the population of the order of 20,000 per year over the whole of London. Change has also occurred in the structure of activities. The manufacturing sector now employs about 328,000 people, a significant reduction from the early 1980s, when nearly 650,000 were employed. Manufacturing is still important to London in employment terms. Economically, however, the services sectors account for around 84% of London's total GDP.

1.21. In land use terms, major change has taken place in parallel with economic restructuring. The physical expansion of the continuous built up area of London was halted by the designation of the Green Belt and the advent of the planning system after the war. Much growth subsequently took place in smaller towns outside London, including a large number of new and expanded towns. The financial centre continued to experience development, assisted by the improvement of radial rail services serving long distance commuters and by the development of telecommunications, whilst some suburban centres grew by becoming office and shopping areas in their own right.

1.22. Decentralisation and the decline of heavy and processing industries have left parts of the capital with worn out buildings, large tracts of derelict land and outdated infrastructure, whilst in some inner Boroughs unemployment exceeds 20%. Much of industrial London was destroyed by the war, and

many enterprises and their workers moved to new locations outside London. Industrial decline has been greatest in north and east London. There has been continuing pressure for development in the west, bolstered by its proximity to Heathrow, but even here there are pockets of decline and deprivation. The result is the existence of large sites for re-development, which in some areas have remained unused for many years. These are found mainly in Docklands, East London and the Lee Valley, as well as Park Royal and the Wandle Valley. These sites need to be brought back into use quickly if land is to be used efficiently and if pressures for development elsewhere in the capital and in the South East are to be reduced.

1.23. It is no coincidence that the distribution of derelict and underused land also tends to mirror that of social and economic deprivation across London. In many areas there is a continuing mismatch between skills and labour market demands, leading to a lack of competitiveness and high unemployment. To tackle these problems the Government is encouraging integrated approaches to regeneration, combining physical improvements with social and employment measures which build on the principles laid down in the Government's competitiveness agenda. In addition to the main programmes of the relevant departments, the Single Regeneration Budget (SRB) supports local partnerships in tackling local problems.

1.24. Training and Enterprise Councils (TECs) are involved in economic development partnerships throughout London in which local authorities, businesses and community organisations are working together to improve their areas. The granting of Assisted Area and European Regional Development Fund Objective 2 status to the areas facing major structural change has given added impetus. Boroughs will need to ensure that their planning activities underpin these partnerships and that there is full consultation on land uses, transport infrastructure and traffic management in areas where local partnerships are active. The first two rounds of the SRB have led to many schemes starting across London. The resulting projects, the City Challenge partnerships and the Housing Action Trusts all need to be encouraged and supported.

1.25. London is competing with other European and world cities for inward investment. A better quality environment, protection for our outstanding heritage and promoting ease of movement are not just desirable for those who live and work in London, but make good economic sense as well. A good quality of life will improve the ability of London to attract the organisations, people and investment which create wealth. A diverse economy, a range of employment opportunities and the pursuit of attractive housing and community facilities will increase the competitiveness of London and encourage more people to participate in its economy rather than to seek opportunities outside its boundaries.

London: a city of opportunity

1.26. The best prospects for employment are expected to remain in the service sector, although it will not be immune from the effects of changing working patterns and organisation. London already has unique strengths in many sectors which are expected to be at the forefront of economic development in the next century; for example, finance and business services, the arts, culture, entertainment, sport and tourism. London will need to provide for the growth which these sectors offer, for example by allowing development in appropriate locations, by encouraging the development of mixed use areas or sites linked either physically or electronically and by improving the accessibility of enterprises to their local, regional, national and international markets. Boroughs will need to deal flexibly with proposals which cut across conventional land use descriptions or which require a greater rate of local change than may have occurred in the recent past.

1.27. The financial sector will continue to be a vital element of the London economy and the Central Area will remain the main focus of the higher order functions associated with it. It will, as now, continue to be supported by a wide range of business services, ranging from accountancy, legal and consultancy services, through telecommunications, media, marketing and promotional services, as well as restaurants, theatres and the arts.

1.28. The estimated value to London of the tourist industry, which is one of the fastest growing sectors in the world, was £6.8 billion in 1995, from some 20 million visitors (both domestic and overseas). Tourism related employment provides over 200,000 jobs as well as supporting many others. London is by far the most important destination for overseas visitors to the UK, 80% of whom arrive via London and a large proportion of whom spend at least one night in the capital. London is therefore the UK's tourism "brand leader", attracting over half of its total visitor revenue. It will, however, only remain so if it maintains its competitiveness and rises to future challenges. It is critical that Boroughs assist this sector by measures designed to improve the quality of visitor accommodation, to encourage hotel development given the existing shortage of hotels, and to create a better environment within which visitors can enjoy London.

1.29. The arts, cultural, and entertainment sectors are vital assets to tourism, as well as being important economic sectors in their own right. They are major contributors to the quality of life of both residents and visitors and as a whole employ some 200,000 people. London, with its concentration of cultural heritage, its unique mix of national, regional and local arts and performance companies, its lively music and theatre sub-culture, its role as home of the UK fashion industry and the creative centre for the media, is a recognised world leader in this field. Much of London's traditional artistic and cultural heritage is concentrated in the Central Area and there is potential for further development both here and beyond, which Boroughs should encourage.

Sustainable development

1.30. Future planning activity must incorporate measures to contribute to a more sustainable future. The principles are set out in the White Paper *This Common Inheritance* (HM Government 1990) and in *Sustainable Development - the UK Strategy* (HM Government 1994a). Chapters 24 to 26 of the Strategy are particularly relevant to development, the built environment and transport. Boroughs should also put their planning activities in the context of local Agenda 21 (the strategy endorsed at the 1992 UN Conference on Environment and Development - the "Earth Summit") and have regard to the Association of London Government's statement on Local Agenda 21 (Association of London Government 1995).

1.31. The land-use planning system is a key instrument in ensuring that development is compatible with the aims of sustainable development. UDPs should demonstrate how planning policies have been framed having regard to these aims and should include an assessment of their likely effects on the environment using an environmental appraisal (Department of the Environment 1993). Further guidance is given in

Chapter 10. In showing how their plans contribute to sustainable development, authorities should explain how their activities encourage the maximum use of existing resources, particularly when these can achieve the goal of fostering and maintaining activity whilst reducing the need for travel, especially by car. Borough planning activity should aim to reduce energy inputs, take account of the need to contribute to reducing emissions of greenhouse gases and air pollution, increase the recycling and reuse of wastes, and minimise the need for waste disposal, especially over long distances.

The role of Strategic Planning Guidance

1.32. This Guidance replaces the first RPG3 published in 1989, which set the strategic land use planning context for Boroughs during the production of the first round of London UDPs. Much of what was contained in the 1989 Guidance is still applicable as Government policy and has been brought forward as appropriate. New guidance is given on issues where policy has evolved or is presented for the first time. Following publication of Draft Revised Guidance in 1995, many helpful

comments were received during the consultation period. The London Pride Partnership has also prepared its prospectus for the future of London (London Pride Partnership 1994). The Secretary of State is grateful for the considerable interest that has been taken in the future of London by its local authorities, businesses, community groups and individuals.

1.33. The Secretary of State regards it as particularly important that London Boroughs (Fig 1.2) follow this Guidance in the preparation of UDPs and in the exercise of their responsibilities for the control of development. London needs up to date, clear and relevant UDPs. Some first round UDPs are still to be completed and the Government hopes that those outstanding will be adopted as soon as possible. Following adoption of these first UDPs, Boroughs must review their plans and bring forward proposals to amend them as soon as practicable to reflect revised Guidance and recent and revised national Planning Policy Guidance Notes (PPGs). This is particularly important in the case of Boroughs where UDPs have been adopted for several years and where they do not fully incorporate the latest policy

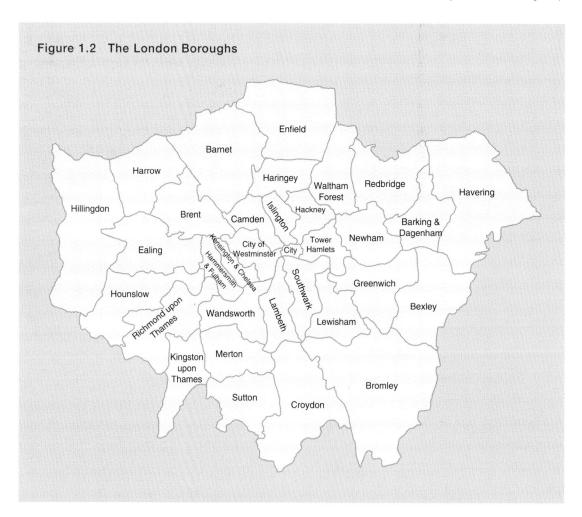

Figure 1.2 The London Boroughs

guidance as set out in PPGs. This Guidance is written to guide UDPs which will set out policies and proposals up to 2006, but also considers opportunities which may occur beyond that date. A note on the role of Guidance in the planning system is given at Appendix 1 and a list of relevant Planning Guidance Notes is at Appendix 4.

Coordination of Planning in London

The Government Office for London

The Government Office for London (GOL), established in April 1994, brings together the four key Departments of Education and Employment, Environment, Trade and Industry, and Transport. Working closely with the Home Office and the Departments for National Heritage and Health to respond to the needs of London, it is committed to maximising the competitiveness, prosperity and quality of life in London in partnership with local people.

The Cabinet Sub-Committee for London

The Cabinet Sub-Committee for London brings together Ministers from Government Departments with responsibilities for London under the Chairmanship of the Secretary of State for the Environment. The role of the Sub-Committee is to coordinate the Government's policies on London.

Joint London Advisory Panel

The Joint London Advisory Panel has been set up by the Secretary of State for the Environment to advise London Ministers on strategic issues of relevance to London. The Panel comprises the nine London Pride Partners and members of the Cabinet Sub-Committee for London. The Panel will meet two or three times a year and short notes of discussions will be made public.

The London Pride Partnership

The London Pride Partnership comprises organisations representing the range of private, public and voluntary sector interests in London and includes London First, the Association of London Government, the London CBI, the London Chamber of Commerce and Industry, the London Planning Advisory Committee, the London Training and Enterprise Councils, the London Voluntary Services Council, the Corporation of London and Westminster City Council.

The London Planning Advisory Committee

The London Planning Advisory Committee (LPAC) is a joint committee of the London Boroughs and the City Corporation in their capacity as the 33 local planning authorities in London. LPAC was established by the 1985 Local Government Act and came into existence in 1986. In broad terms its statutory functions are to advise both Government and London's 33 local planning authorities on the strategic land use and transport planning of the capital; to take part on London's behalf in South East regional planning; and to advise the Government on parking policy for London.

LPAC's functions are set out in full in Section 5 of the Local Government Act 1985, Section 3 of the Town and Country Planning Act 1990 and Section 63 of the Road Traffic Act 1991.

2. A Strategic Framework for London's Development and Regeneration

DEVELOPMENT AND REGENERATION

2.1. This chapter sets out the strategic framework which forms the basis of the Government's economic development strategy for regeneration and partnership action. Boroughs should have regard to it in exercising their planning and economic development responsibilities and review their UDPs to include appropriate policies and proposals.

2.2. The economic and geographical structure of London is complex and it is not possible to divide it into rigid sub areas. There is, however, a clear underlying spatial pattern and structure to its economic activity and opportunities. The Secretary of State considers that this should provide the framework for new development, growth and regeneration activities. It reflects and consolidates the pattern of regeneration initiatives which the Government has sponsored in London, which comprise in particular three Assisted Areas, the East London and Lee Valley Objective 2 area, City Challenges, and successful Single Regeneration Budget (SRB) Partnerships. The key components of the framework are the Central Area and its margins, major zones of economic activity and development opportunity, the Thames and town centres.

2.3. **The Central Area** provides a focus for London's world city, capital and metropolitan functions based around the two cores of the Cities of London and Westminster. It is critical to the prosperity of London as a whole that the Central Area can continue to accommodate the evolving demands of London's metropolitan and world city role. Land use planning will need to ensure that London continues to attract the high order service functions which make it a successful world city today. Business and commerce will need to have access to the latest developments in building technology and quality. At the same time, the distinctive character of the City, the West End, and the other quarters within the Central Area need to be preserved, its residential role sustained, and development balanced against proper and increasing demands for improvements in the quality of life and sustainability. In contrast to the Central Area itself, its margins to the north, east and across the river to the south contain the remnants of London's traditional industrial quarters, residential communities, including many of the most deprived people in the country, and a series of large scale areas of vacant and underused land which represent central London's major opportunities for new development and growth. The Central Area margins need to consolidate their existing economic strengths and develop new economic roles. The major development sites in the margins need to be brought forward for development that can rebuild the local urban structure, define a new image for their areas, extend Central Area uses where appropriate and bring benefits to their local communities. Major international termini at King's Cross/St. Pancras, Paddington and Waterloo are particularly significant. A considered extension of Central Area uses across the River Thames can both strengthen London's world city role and assist with the regeneration of the South Bank.

2.4. **The major zones of economic activity and development opportunity** fan out from the centre and in some cases extend without interruption to the edge of the metropolis along historic transport routes. These are the homes of London's industrial traditions and still contain the major concentrations of its manufacturing and business activity outside central London. The efficient functioning of these areas to meet modern business requirements and attract new development to underutilised sites is of primary importance to London's regeneration. The most prominent corridor is the Thames Gateway, to the east. It contains much of London's vacant land and the majority of its large scale development opportunities. The Lee Valley, to the north, contains a significant proportion of London's remaining manufacturing activity. The Wandle Valley is the focus of manufacturing activity and development land in south London. The pattern in west London is not dominated by any single corridor but nevertheless contains clearly defined areas of strategic economic importance which are focused on main arterial transport routes, notably Park Royal.

2.5. To the east and west, superimposed upon this pattern, lie respectively **Canary Wharf** and **Heathrow**, each an increasing influence on it's local economy and that of London as a whole. Canary Wharf, developed in concert with the Lower Lea, Royal Docks and Stratford can serve to reshape radically the image and economic potential of this part of east London. Heathrow is steadily becoming the dominant factor in the economy of south-west London, attracting activity which creates development pressure on new sites while pockets of established industry remain underutilised. These older areas need to be restructured to accommodate pressures generated within the local economy. Strategic public transport improvements can serve to widen Heathrow's area of benefit to embrace more of the capital's areas of deprivation.

2.6. **The Thames** has historically defined the southern extent of the Central Area and further eastward provided the location for some of London's major industries and large scale users of land. The decline and departure of these industries, notably the London Docks, has left behind major problems of dereliction and an area of change extending to the margins of the Central Area and incorporating the South Bank as far as Vauxhall. Historically representing a barrier to movement, the river can increasingly be seen as a positive new context for future development and regeneration. London's broader river and canal system, which for historical reasons corresponds closely to its pattern of economic activity, also offers scope for regeneration strategies which can link economic development to environmental objectives.

2.7. **Town centres** provide the focal points around which civic life and many local services are structured, and can be major centres of employment and growth, particularly in areas which lie outside the major zones of activity identified above. The role of town centres is explained in Chapter 5.

Regeneration and development

2.8. London's economic structure is undergoing change. New opportunities for growth and development are taking shape as traditional activities have declined. As a result clear differences have emerged between east and west London, and inner and outer London in the pattern of economic activity, levels of prosperity, economic competitiveness and development opportunity.

2.9. London contains the largest concentration of deprivation in the UK and parts of London now contain some of the most deprived communities in the country. These focus in particular on inner east London and inner south London, though distinct areas exist also in parts of west London and in outer London, particularly in peripheral post-war housing estates. There is considerable variation across the capital, both between Boroughs and also within them, as in many parts of London conditions vary substantially from one small area to another (see Fig 2.1). Measures of deprivation have indicated a deterioration between the 1981 and 1991 censuses in the position of London, particularly parts of outer London, in relation to other parts of the UK. London has clearly suffered from the effects of the last recession.

2.10. Jobs have been lost in manufacturing and for unskilled manual work and it is the areas which have been traditionally reliant on these sectors that have been particularly affected. This process has left many of London's major economic areas increasingly uncompetitive, characterised by ageing business infrastructure and large areas of vacant and underused land. This situation is particularly pronounced in east London, in the Thames Gateway and Lee Valley corridors, and overlaps many of the capital's most deprived areas.

2.11. A key objective for regeneration in London is to reduce these imbalances in its prosperity by creating the necessary conditions to enable the less favoured areas to compete more successfully for new investment, harness the surplus capacity of their areas and their resources of vacant land, and exploit in particular the opportunities offered by new access to Europe and the centre. Redevelopment and regeneration should be encouraged through targeted action in impoverished and run down areas. The existing economic strengths and major development opportunities present, particularly in East London and the Central Area margins, need to be realised in ways which will provide durable new employment opportunities that can diversify both their local economies and the economy of London as a whole. These opportunities need to be made accessible to those living and working in neighbouring areas so that the local labour force, local suppliers and supporting enterprises, including small businesses, can benefit from the growth.

FOCAL POINTS FOR REGENERATION

2.12.   London's corridors and the Central Area margins provide the key strategic opportunities in the capital to provide more competitive locations for business, to attract and nurture new economic sectors, to secure the development of vacant and underused land and to bring forward new investment opportunities. Investment in strategic road and rail infrastructure is consolidating the regeneration and development potential of these areas. The evolving transport network, aligned to the pattern of existing economic activity and development opportunity in the corridors, is serving to define a series of focal points for new development that can attract new investment and provide employment opportunities for local people (see Map 2). Boroughs should work together and with other parties in partnership to prepare strategies which adopt an integrated approach to transport and development at the local level. Strategies should build on the particular strengths of the different locations, identifying key opportunities and improving accessibility to areas of high unemployment and need. They should exploit planned investment in transport infrastructure and encourage new public transport proposals. Improving the environmental quality and image of the corridors is also important, taking full advantage of natural assets including water and open space, and working towards patterns of development and movement which contribute to sustainable development.

2.13.   Potential sites for new development need to be made more attractive to new forms of industry or mixed use development. A limited number of sites should be safeguarded for employment use, as set out in Chapter 3. Policies for mixed use should discourage cross commuting by car which adds to congestion, air pollution and the wasteful use of energy. This may be complemented by measures and policies for parking, traffic management and public transport.

Areas of deprivation

2.14.   The areas of greatest need require comprehensive programmes targeted to improving their social infrastructure, raising the quality of life of their residents and improving accessibility to the employment, cultural and leisure opportunities which London has to offer. Local strategies may be targeted on large housing estates or on focal points such as town centres. They may involve a range of initiatives determined by the circumstances of the area concerned and include housing, environment, training and education programmes, local transport

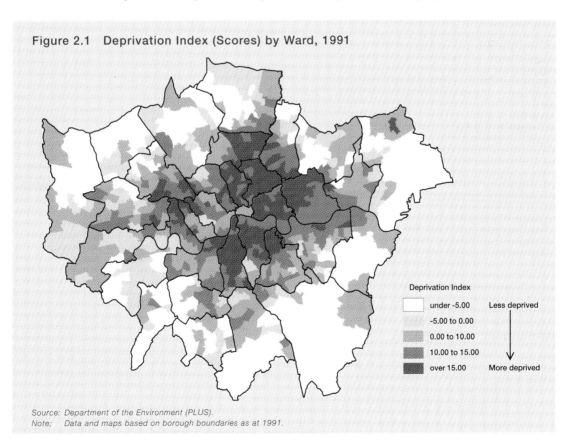

Figure 2.1   Deprivation Index (Scores) by Ward, 1991

Deprivation Index

under -5.00	Less deprived
-5.00 to 0.00	
0.00 to 10.00	
10.00 to 15.00	
over 15.00	More deprived

Source: Department of the Environment (PLUS).
Note;   Data and maps based on borough boundaries as at 1991.

initiatives, crime prevention and projects targeted towards the needs of ethnic minorities. They should be based on a thorough assessment of the area's strengths and weaknesses. Boroughs should pursue packages of measures with TECs and others which both meet local needs and respond to opportunities. They should formulate policies and proposals reflecting the specific local forms and/or combinations of disadvantages in their areas.

Indices of Deprivation

Deprivation is a complex phenomenon. Because pockets of deprivation can exist within otherwise affluent areas, and vice-versa, analysis may need to be carried out at varying spatial scales down to Census Enumeration District level. The DoE's publication *"1991 Deprivation Index: A review of approaches and a matrix of results"* (Department of the Environment 1995a) provides a useful aid to interpretation.

Composite indicators may be used to explore issues of potential multiple deprivation. DoE's 1991 Index of Local Conditions combines a number of indicators, chosen to cover a range of economic, social, housing and environmental issues, into a single deprivation score for each area. At the ward level (Fig 2.1), the indicators are unemployment, children in low earning households, overcrowded housing, housing lacking basic amenities, households with no car, children in 'unsuitable' accommodation, and educational participation at age 17. The indicators are standardised, transformed, and then summed, all indicators having an equal weight in the index. Scores of zero indicate an area at the national (England) norm, with positive scores indicating relatively high levels of deprivation and negative scores indicating relatively low levels of deprivation.

Authorities should also be prepared to use sub-indices (e.g. for housing, and economic/labour-market/poverty issues), or individual indicators where relevant to the policy issues under consideration.

The role of partnerships

2.15.   This range of problems presents a challenge which cannot be addressed by Boroughs acting in isolation.   A key feature of the Government's regeneration strategy is the development of joint local

partnerships to develop and deliver clearly coordinated local strategies, appropriate to the characteristics of the area concerned. Partnerships between the Boroughs, TECs, landowners, investors, local businesses and the voluntary sector have been successful in winning funding for a variety of regeneration schemes. Partnership should involve full consultation with the local community, agencies and organisations.   There is scope to cultivate the growing awareness of local needs and opportunities which will benefit, for example, the consultation process of development plan preparation and discussions on Local Agenda 21.

2.16.   TECs (Fig 2.2) are the Government's key private sector partners in local development and have two important roles to play.   First, they ensure effective private sector leadership within economic partnerships by contributing to the development of local strategies and growth targets and by levering in private finance. Second, TECs contribute directly to the implementation of local strategies to enhance the competitiveness of people and businesses through their skills training and enterprise support provision.   They should be closely involved in local employment regeneration strategies.

Figure 2.2   The London Training and Enterprise Councils (TECs)

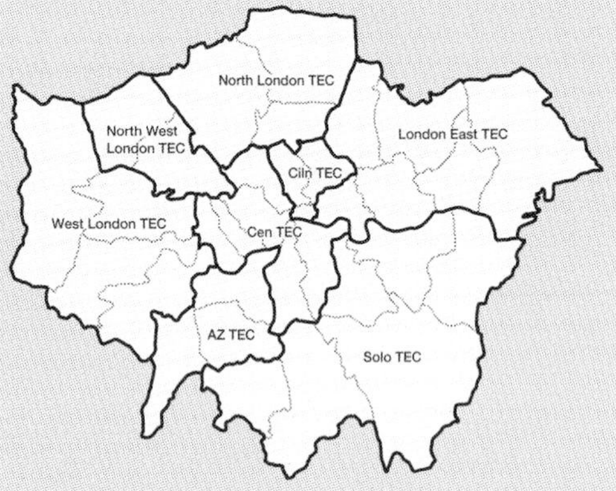

Source: Government Office for London.

Role of the UDP

2.17.   There should be a clear and direct interrelationship between the UDP and regeneration programmes and priorities. Regeneration strategies which involve new development should be based on a clear planning framework.   Proposals for sites should have regard to the nature of the surrounding area, existing infrastructure together with the potential for site improvements, and information on the likely land requirements for future uses. There should be a clear policy indication of the likely acceptable land uses and, where appropriate, specific proposals in the UDP. Under the development plan led system, promoters of regeneration activities and bidders for funds must have regard to the policies and proposals set out in UDPs. It is therefore important that UDPs facilitate the development of appropriate regeneration strategies and are kept up to date to incorporate progress on regeneration activities and partnerships.

2.18. Boroughs should:

- work cooperatively with neighbouring authorities, LPAC and other appropriate bodies to prepare strategic policies for development and regeneration, recognising the opportunities for investment in transport infrastructure and the need for joint action to tackle London's problems

- have regard to local indicators of need and deprivation and consider what policies are required to tackle problems

- define areas where resources need to be concentrated to create a better environment and provide employment opportunities

- consider how transport and land use can be linked together to improve accessibility to opportunities for all and to deliver more sustainable patterns of development in regenerated areas

- provide a context in plans for partnership activity and a firm land use basis for regeneration by setting out positive policies and proposals for development (Non-planning considerations, such as the management of regeneration or details of partnership arrangements should, where relevant, form part of the reasoned justification for policies and proposals.)

- encourage mixed use development through policies and proposals by setting criteria for controls on land uses to meet the needs of different areas and by responding flexibly to changes in local circumstances.

A strategic approach to development

2.19. The following sections provide information on the main areas of development and regeneration in London. They should be read together with the guidance on separate topics provided in subsequent chapters. Central London and its margins and the main corridors of regeneration are expected to be the main priorities for action and physical change over the life of this Guidance, where policies and proposals need to be agreed by several Boroughs and reflected in their UDPs. There are other areas and sites which will be important, but on a geographically smaller scale. Figure 2.3 shows the distribution of manufacturing employment as a percentage of all employment at ward level across London.

2.20. Boroughs should:

- implement the structural framework presented in this chapter when reviewing plans and assessing development proposals

- consider what other areas need concerted action to facilitate development and improve the environment, and present policies and proposals accordingly.

CENTRAL LONDON AND ITS MARGINS

Central London

2.21. Central London is a world business and commercial centre, but one which also provides cultural, retail, tourism and other services which are of national and international significance. The Central Area contains the historic core of the capital and many of the features which define London's image, including ceremonial, state, historical and traditional locations and activities. The area also contains a significant residential population which contributes to the life and character of London, as well as including elements of the workforce vital to the centre's economic and other functions. Boroughs, when reviewing UDPs, should recognise the importance of all these activities and make proper allowance for them.

2.22. Boroughs and other agencies should work together to improve the quality of the activities and attractions in the centre. During the lifetime of this Guidance many organisations in central London will be promoting major activities and developments to

Figure 2.3 Employment in Manufacturing as % of Total Employment at Ward Level

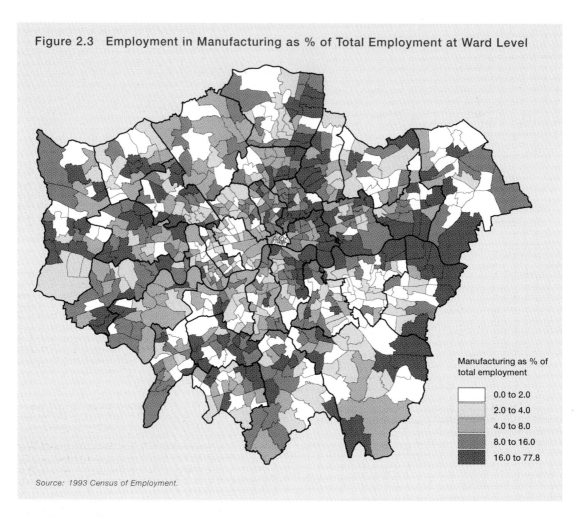

Manufacturing as % of
total employment

	0.0 to 2.0
	2.0 to 4.0
	4.0 to 8.0
	8.0 to 16.0
	16.0 to 77.8

Source: 1993 Census of Employment.

celebrate the Millennium. Planning policies should promote and facilitate these and developers and other agencies should consider how their actions might bring forward suitable development to enhance London's standing and be of lasting benefit.

2.23. Historically, central London has been delineated as the area between the main railway termini although different bodies tend to use different working definitions. Boroughs have tended to take different approaches to the definition of areas within central London and the review of plans should achieve greater consistency. Boroughs should therefore review their own definitions in the light of the description given in this Guidance. They should, with LPAC, agree on the criteria to be adopted to define central functions and ensure that definitions are consistent across Borough boundaries. For data collection purposes, as continuity over time is important, the Central Statistical Area boundary should be retained in parallel if necessary with other agreed boundaries for analysis of current policy concerns.

2.24. The Secretary of State considers that a realistic

definition of the Central Area extends from Kensington and Knightsbridge in the west to Whitechapel in the east and from Marylebone and King's Cross in the north to the South Bank between Vauxhall and Tower Bridge. This area is shown on Map 3. It covers the whole of the City of London and parts of the City of Westminster and the Boroughs of Camden, Hackney, Islington, Kensington and Chelsea, Lambeth, Southwark and Tower Hamlets. In the light of this Guidance, Boroughs should agree on a detailed definition of the Central Area which should be justified in each UDP and shown on Proposals Maps.

2.25. It is important that policies for the Central Area as a whole are compatible across Borough boundaries. To that end, UDPs should contain policies for it and explain how cross Borough issues have been resolved. Boroughs will be expected to present policies in a way that enables users to compare policies across boundaries. They should therefore agree, in consultation with LPAC, a common presentation for illustrative material and their Proposals Maps. LPAC are asked to monitor policies for this area and to report regularly to

A Broad Description of Areas Within Central London

The City of London and the area close to its boundaries is likely to remain the most appropriate location for major office activity, particularly for financial services.

The West End contains major offices, particularly high quality head offices, but in association with a wider range of retail, entertainment, cultural, residential and supporting facilities. The area around Oxford Street contains the greatest concentration of shopping in the UK, and the area around Shaftesbury Avenue the main concentration of theatres. The implementation of safeguarded transport schemes would enhance the West End's accessibility.

The main concentration of universities extends from the Strand and Aldwych through Bloomsbury to the Euston Road, while specialised arts, entertainment, restaurant and retail facilities have developed in Soho, Covent Garden and the area north of Oxford Street.

The main centres of Government and Royalty are located between Whitehall and Victoria.

The area known as "Midtown" is centred on Farringdon, which could gain from increased accessibility by rail services to much of Greater London and beyond. There is likely to be considerable scope for redevelopment or refurbishment following the removal of much of "Fleet Street" to other locations, including Docklands, and opportunities to redevelop or adapt under used office space for other uses requiring good accessibility.

The northern fringes of the City contain the majority of London's specialised quarters, including jewellery and precision industries in Hatton Garden and Clerkenwell, together with a growing interest in residential units and developments combining living and working space.

The Royal Parks, Great Estates and London Squares are highly distinctive, offering urban landscape of outstanding quality and reinforcing London's image as a pleasant city.

A western residential fringe stretches from Bayswater through Kensington to Chelsea and Pimlico. This area is comparatively prosperous and contains important retail, cultural and educational facilities, including Kensington, Knightsbridge, Sloane Square, the Kings Road, the Albert Hall and the South Kensington museums complex.

The South Bank arts centre is Europe's largest arts centre and the area from Westminster Bridge to Blackfriars Bridge has considerable further development potential, especially with its proximity to the Waterloo International Terminal. Bankside has several regeneration opportunities, including the Globe Theatre and the reuse of the former power station as the new Tate Gallery of Modern Art.

The centre contains several other universities and centres of learning. These have an important influence on the activities of the surrounding areas and, like the major teaching and specialist hospitals and places of worship, act as focal points for users and visitors. Nearby locations are often suitable for student and nurses accommodation which could be a good way of re-establishing high density living and bringing residential life to parts of the centre.

Boroughs and the Secretary of State on the main planning issues.

2.26. The Secretary of State considers that there are certain non residential activities which are particularly appropriate in the Central Area. A list of these is given in Table 2.1. However, central London is not, and should not be, homogeneous. Different uses will predominate in different parts, and this variety should be supported. In particular, although office uses should remain concentrated in the Central Area, especially within walking distance of the main railway termini and stations, offices should not predominate everywhere. Other activities are traditionally associated with different locations and developments reinforcing the character of these

areas should be encouraged, whilst in specific locations with a distinctive residential character, intrusive new office developments may need to be discouraged.

2.27. It is essential that the Central Area includes housing for those who wish to live in it and for those who need to live in close proximity to their work. Housing and supporting services are key central London activities and should be accorded equal importance to the more specific central activities. There are clear opportunities to provide housing for higher income groups. However, affordable housing also needs to be given particular attention, as many service workers on whom the central functions depend, require accommodation in areas which may not be affordable by reason of high land values and competing uses. There may be scope for the use of redundant or vacant office buildings, or sites with unimplemented planning permissions for offices, to provide different types of housing in suitable locations. In view of the high levels of public transport accessibility and the availability of shops and other facilities, it will not be necessary for every residence to have a parking space. Boroughs should not require minimum residential parking standards where they would make conversion of buildings impractical or where they would lead to lower densities than would be typical for central city living.

Table 2.1 Appropriate Non Residential Activities for Central London

- Those connected with the State and Government
- Diplomatic representations including Embassies, High Commissions and Agencies
- National and international headquarters and associated offices connected with finance, trade, business, professional bodies, institutions and associations
- Facilities and establishments connected with the communications, publishing, advertising, media and cultural sectors of regional, national and international importance
- Shopping, including specialist retail outlets of regional, national and international importance
- Centres of excellence for higher education and research
- Medical establishments of regional, national and international importance
- Legal and professional services
- Arts, culture and entertainment, including museums, art galleries, libraries, theatres, concert halls and cinemas of regional, national and international importance
- Specialist industrial clusters associated with other central activities, including clothing, fashion trades, printing and retail services
- Churches and other religious centres and places of assembly of regional, national and international importance
- Tourism facilities including hotels and conference centres
- Transport facilities, particularly for public transport of regional, national and international importance
- Activities supporting the use and enjoyment of the River Thames
- Other uses providing essential support services and facilities for people living, working and visiting central London.

2.28. UDPs should encourage a broad base of mixed land uses and employment opportunities. These uses will include residential, retail, hotels, arts, culture and entertainment, education and health. Boroughs should also consider how they propose to make adequate provision for local businesses, services and specialist uses. Specific areas may be identified in UDPs where particular policies are necessary to preserve continuing vitality and viability or pattern of existing activities. Traditional economic quarters within central London and its margins should be considered in this regard. Clear planning policies are required which balance the opportunities for commercial development against the need to provide for a thriving and vibrant residential sector and facilities for visitors. The aim should be to maintain and improve the attractive and unique character of central London, without restricting development that contributes to London's world city role.

2.29. High standards should be sought in the design and construction of new development. These should respect the heritage and needs of conservation but, where appropriate, opportunities should be taken for new and innovative design which enhances the urban environment. The siting of prominent buildings should be considered carefully and strategic views protected. Important local views and criteria to identify areas or groups of buildings worthy of protection should be identified in UDPs. It will also be appropriate for Boroughs to identify in UDPs specific areas which make important contributions to the character of London, or which contain important specialist uses. Examples are the Chinatown area of Soho, Covent Garden and Savile Row.

2.30. Central London is the focus of the nation's transport system and the dense network of public transport serving the rest of London and the South East Region. The promotion of public transport accessibility to the Central Area is vital for London as a world city, to support tourism and the main activities of the West End and the City. Existing public transport access is good and investment in radial lines will enhance it, for example the investment that will take place on the Northern Line.

In order to promote the objectives of sustainable development and improve the quality of the environment, development in the Central Area should be primarily served by public transport and not be dependent on the car. Non-residential parking should be limited to essential operational needs.

2.31. Wherever possible, opportunities should be taken to enhance the street scene and encourage walking and cycling, together with safe and convenient access to public transport stops and stations. Given the emphasis on public transport and high pedestrian flows, it should be possible to restrict car access and to increase the space devoted to pedestrians. Traffic management and environmental improvement will be particularly important where activities are facing growing competition from purpose designed facilities elsewhere, for example Oxford Street which is facing competition from out of centre regional shopping facilities.

2.32. There may be locations where developments can make a significant contribution to the infrastructure of central London, by improving interchange facilities or contributing directly to major improvements of the public transport system. This will be of particular value in those locations where new or enhanced rail services are in prospect. Examples are the Jubilee Line extension, which is at present under construction and Thameslink 2000. Other possible projects are CrossRail and the Chelsea-Hackney Line, though these schemes will depend on the availability of public and private finance. Sites within the Central Area include:

- Victoria, where links to Gatwick and proximity to the West End and Whitehall/Westminster, together with rebuilt coach facilities, make this an important interchange

- the proposed stations on CrossRail, particularly around Farringdon which would, with Thameslink 2000, lie at the point of intersection of two regional rail lines serving much of south east England, as well as Heathrow, Gatwick and Luton airports. The existing Thameslink line already serves Farringdon, however the caveat above about the uncertainty of finance and thus of timing for large new rail projects is of particular relevance here. Land use change in the past and recent movement of activity away from this part of the City means that there is considerable

potential for development in the medium to longer term.

The Central Area margins

2.33. The Central Area broadly marks the extent of the pre-Victorian city, while the area outside was developed during the period of intense industrialisation and the expansion of trade and Empire. Many major space users, once generating considerable activity, have become redundant. The sites of railway yards, depots, power stations, canal basins and markets present opportunities but there are often practical difficulties in securing new uses on them. They represent a major regeneration resource which can complement or enhance nearby Central Area functions and act as a magnet for inward investment, while at the same time contributing to meeting local needs. Existing economic strengths of these areas, for example traditional economic quarters which still remain and activities serving the Central Area, need to be consolidated and new economic roles, for example in cultural industries, leisure and tourism need to be developed.

2.34. The Central Area margins contain some of the most severe pockets of deprivation in the country. Comprehensive strategies are required to raise the quality of life in these areas and improve the community's accessibility to the employment, cultural and leisure opportunities which London has to offer. A balance needs to be struck between the potential of these areas to extend the influence of the centre and the prospect of increased land values and demand squeezing out local and long established enterprises, thereby further weakening the communities. The most successful regeneration schemes will be those which add to London's overall critical mass in its world city functions but which contribute to meeting the needs of all sections of the community. A similar balance will need to be struck between the potential demand for higher value residential development, taking advantage of the proximity to the Central Area and the need for affordable dwellings.

2.35. The UDP should be the vehicle for setting out the proposed balance between competing demands and providing opportunity for public debate and consultation to reconcile the different interests. It should establish a clear set of priorities for the development and use of land and for the integration of transport schemes with development.

Boroughs should demonstrate in their reviews of UDPs that they have considered the potential of the main areas of opportunity and prepared proposals for them. The reasoned justification should explain any partnership arrangements and show that neighbouring authorities have been consulted.

2.36. Major development opportunities will arise in areas near to the international transport interchanges of King's Cross, Paddington and Waterloo. All should accommodate proposals for a mixture of land uses. The highest densities and most commercial uses should be closest to the termini. These may include large offices, drawing on the high accessibility to regional and international networks, subject to there being a reasonable prospect of demand (see Chapter 3). Away from the sites of highest accessibility, clear attempts should be made to promote uses which support and regenerate local communities, providing both residential and associated uses and community facilities serving the needs of both new development and established neighbouring areas.

2.37. The main areas are:

- King's Cross. The scale and location of the former railway lands, adjoining the proposed Channel Tunnel Rail Link (CTRL) terminus at St Pancras and situated within one of the most deprived areas of London, gives it particular metropolitan significance. Its catchment area could be enhanced by domestic services on the CTRL, and by the proposed Thameslink 2000 services, which will, in addition to the existing services on the Midland Main Line (including improved interchange facilities for Luton Airport) and West Anglia Great Northern Lines, include enhanced access through the City to Gatwick, South London, Surrey and Sussex. Proposals should be brought forward for a new quarter of London with a distinctive identity, enhancing features of historic and conservation importance. There will be scope for development for business, tourism and leisure, including areas of high density uses. It will be appropriate to provide housing and community facilities and measures to enhance access to employment which benefit neighbouring local communities

- Paddington. The location of the terminus of the Heathrow Express, due to open in 1998, means that this area will become a gateway to central

London from Heathrow Airport. Proposals should have regard to the need to consider local transport movement and to improve the environment, both in the vicinity of the station and in the surrounding communities. Further opportunities could arise with the development of CrossRail giving rapid links to both east and west, including greatly increased accessibility to the City

- Bishopsgate/Spitalfields. This area contains many large scale redundant buildings and sites and would benefit from the improved public transport access of the proposed East London Line Extension. The area is capable of accommodating a high quality mixed urban environment serving the City, the distinct commercial area of Spitalfields and Aldgate and the growing cultural quarters in Shoreditch. There will be opportunities for higher density mixed use schemes, including both residential and commercial development, but respect will need to be shown to the historic character and rich ethnic diversity which it contains

- the South Bank. The riverside, from the former docklands of Bermondsey in the east as far as Nine Elms in the west, is undergoing substantial change throughout its length. It holds a particularly important position in London's geography, fronting the Thames and possessing a Central Area dimension, whilst containing well-established local communities. The area's accessibility will be enhanced by the Jubilee Line Extension, with stations at Waterloo, Southwark, London Bridge, and Bermondsey, and other improved cross river pedestrian and rail links are under consideration. A series of focal points can be distinguished: Bermondsey Riverside, Pool of London, Bankside, the South Bank arts complex and Waterloo, and Vauxhall/Nine Elms. Partnerships have been established to progress their regeneration and the development of better cross river links. Waterloo particularly can benefit from the combination of the International Terminal and improved metropolitan links with the Jubilee Line Extension, coupled with the proximity to the established arts and cultural quarter at the South Bank complex. There is scope to extend Central Area activities, particularly in the fields of business, leisure and tourism, to enhance the use of the river and to provide new business opportunities and employment for the local population.

LONDON'S REGENERATION CORRIDORS

Thames Gateway

2.38. That part of the Thames Gateway in London, extending from Stratford and the Royal Docks to the M25, contains London's largest development sites. The *Thames Gateway Planning Framework* (RPG9A) has set out a broad development strategy defining the key principles to be applied to secure the regeneration of the area. Boroughs should incorporate these principles into reviews of UDPs. In addition, during the period of this Guidance UDPs will cover the area for which the London Docklands Development Corporation (LDDC) has hitherto had planning responsibilities. Boroughs should include appropriate policies and proposals in future UDPs.

2.39. Areas of opportunity are set out in more detail in the Planning Framework. On the north bank these comprise the Royal Docks and Beckton, Barking Reach and Havering Riverside, which are for the most part large scale redundant land poorly integrated into the neighbouring area to the north. A key strategic goal is to improve their integration, in terms of access and urban structure, with the urban hinterland. The value of the City Airport will be enhanced by improving links to Canary Wharf, Stratford and the City, while in the Royal Victoria Dock there are proposals for a major exhibition and event centre. The provision of enhanced public transport connections to these sites, so that much of the movement demand can be met without access to private transport, would help to ensure the success of development schemes in these locations. On the south side regeneration is linked more directly to a string of existing industrial and residential areas and historic town centres which abut the river at Erith, Woolwich, Greenwich, Deptford and Thamesmead. Woolwich has the potential for imaginative development at the historic Royal Arsenal, which could attract many users and visitors, while Greenwich would be well placed to capitalise on its historic sites and meridian associations. The siting of the Millenium Exhibition at Greenwich Peninsula will provide significant regeneration opportunities, which will capitalise on the new Jubilee Line Extension station.

2.40. The promotion of public transport with selective road improvements will aid future economic growth. The strategic road network, with the projects already in hand, is largely complete. Strategic rail access will be radically enhanced by the new domestic and international passenger station at Stratford, supported by the Jubilee Line Extension. Already the Docklands Light Railway, including the Beckton extension, has formed the backbone of the inner part of the Thames Gateway north of the river. Its catchment will be consolidated by the Lewisham extension. Bus links will be important, as will the development of light rail opportunities as development proceeds east of Docklands.

2.41. *The Thames Gateway Planning Framework* emphasises the importance of providing new and improved cross river links in east London if the area is to function more efficiently and fulfil its development potential. New crossings would give regeneration sites in the eastern Thames Gateway a competitive level of accessibility that would not only help to attract residents and employers, but also retain those that are already there. The environmental disbenefits of congestion arising from insufficient cross river capacity give rise to the need for improvements, but also highlight the problems which may arise if any new road capacity simply accommodates the current suppressed demand.

2.42. The Government has consulted with local community and business interests on how to develop river crossings to the east of Tower Bridge. This indicated strong support for a coherent crossing strategy, providing a balanced approach to land use and transport, that will help the area function more efficiently by linking up complementary land uses more directly and by redressing imbalances between the supply of labour and places of work. However, in order to be sustainable, the strategy must moderate demand for road transport. Meeting regeneration objectives within the area will require some increases in road capacity but the Government will encourage alternative modes through the use of mixed mode transport links combining public transport and good quality cycle and pedestrian routes. This requires a coordinated approach between local authorities, public transport operators and central government. The package of schemes to be developed crossing the river will reflect this approach, particularly a rail tunnel to serve Woolwich, a local multi-modal crossing at Gallions Reach and the third crossing at Blackwall, allowing local transport to use the older existing bore.

2.43. UDPs should reflect and inform the proposals by partnerships to improve the Gateway area. A pattern of regeneration initiatives is now taking shape at both the strategic and local level. A cross borough strategic partnership has been established to pursue issues of strategic importance to the Thames Gateway in London. At the local level, in addition to the LDDC's responsibility for the Royal Docks, a series of SRB strategies are targeting the majority of the key locations, especially Stratford, Canning Town, East Thameside, Woolwich Town Centre and the Arsenal, Greenwich Waterfront and Deptford Creek. Each area has significant opportunities that should be guided by policies and proposals in the relevant UDP.

Stratford, the Thames Gateway Western Focus and Canary Wharf

2.44. Canary Wharf and its associated area of commercial activity and development in the Isle of Dogs have become strategic features of the economic structure of London. The area is destined to complement central London and strengthen the capital's world city role. As a result of the transport networks linking Canary Wharf to its surrounding area, particularly to Stratford, Lewisham and the Royal Docks, there is scope to expand the area of benefit arising from the investment centred on the Isle of Dogs to embrace a much wider area. The opening of the Jubilee Line Extension will radically improve accessibility to central London and to rail services from the region.

2.45. Stratford occupies a pivotal position in the geography of east London. It is already highly accessible to Docklands and the City, and this will improve further with the completion of the Jubilee Line Extension. There is also potential to develop rail services to the Lee Valley and beyond. The development of the domestic and international passenger station and the Channel Tunnel Rail Link will add a new dimension to the accessibility of the area and its attractiveness for development. The existence of a major rail and transport interchange and extensive redundant railway lands will foster regeneration. Over 130 acres of land is available, offering a range of town centre, riverside and parkland locations for development.

2.46. The areas of development opportunity are described in the Thames Gateway Planning Framework. Collectively they could attract a mix of new multi-site commercial, higher education, research and technological innovation, exhibition, cultural and leisure development that could radically reshape the image and potential of inner East London and generate new employment opportunities for the established population of the area. Important heritage sites, for example Greenwich, and the availability of large sites with considerable potential in the Royal Docks and Greenwich Peninsular should provide opportunities for large scale development. This should be linked to the promotion of high capacity public transport to complement the infrastructure which is already being put in place. There remains a need for local road improvements, although, as the area develops, it is intended that the modal split for journeys to work should move more decisively towards public transport.

East London and the Lee Valley

2.47. The area designated under ERDF Objective 2 represents a union between London's traditional East End, in Tower Hamlets, Hackney and Newham, and the 16 mile Lee Valley Corridor which connects the rural edge of London and the M25 to the River Thames. The corridor contains the largest concentration of manufacturing businesses in London, grouped in a series of large industrial estates interspersed with large tracts of potential development land, open space and water systems. The River Lee, which extends the whole length of the corridor, and the Lee Valley Regional Park, which accompanies the river almost the full distance, provide a strategic environmental asset of great value. Regeneration needs to go hand in hand with the enhancement of this significant environmental area, so that development can take place within the context of an attractive and improving environment.

2.48. There are a series of key regeneration locations along the corridor, including major manufacturing locations in need of restructuring and renewal, and opportunity locations for new development that can diversify the economic base and land use pattern of the area. These key locations are Enfield Northern Gateway, Edmonton Corridor, Tottenham Hale, Stratford and Temple Mills and the Lower Lea - the latter two also being located within the boundary of the Thames Gateway. Each has distinctive attributes which can contribute to an integrated development strategy for the area and in particular provide an opportunity to introduce new high quality development, including potential for a science/technology park at Enfield Northern Gateway, a new commercial area at the interchange of the A406 and A1055 at Edmonton and waterside development opportunities at Tottenham Hale attractive to high tech, leisure and business uses.

2.49. The Corridor is flanked at its southern end by a complex and high density mixture of residential communities and local town centres, interlaced with locally significant small employment areas. This will require careful management to improve its residential quality whilst sustaining the economic subcentres of greatest importance. Public transport should be used to give the community access to employment opportunities both locally and more generally in east London.

2.50. East London and the Lee Valley area also has a strategic partnership in place, together with a series of local initiatives, built upon the opportunity provided by the SRB at the Upper Lee, Lea Bridge Gateway, Leytonstone, Stratford and Temple Mills, Hackney, the Lower Lea and Canning Town. In addition, the area contains three City Challenge Partnerships at Dalston, Stratford and Bethnal Green.

West London corridors

2.51. The pattern of economic development in west London is far more dispersed than the two distinctive corridors to the east. Nevertheless, it possesses several concentrations of economic activity, especially around the road, rail and canal corridors which form west London's historic arterial transport network. Park Royal, the largest area, is complemented by a series of industrial and commercial areas forming an arc across west London, of which Cricklewood, Wembley Park, Hayes/West Drayton, Feltham/Hatton Cross and Brentford and the Great West Road are particularly significant for regeneration. Heathrow is the major employment attraction in west London, as is airport related development, embracing distribution, high tech industry, offices and tourism. Pressure for such development will remain strong, whatever decision is reached on the need for a fifth terminal at Heathrow itself.

2.52. Despite the long term need to readjust the economic balance between west and east London, the west London economy is of fundamental regional and national importance. In common with east London, the established corridors of economic activity are in need of restructuring and renewal to sustain their vital role and should be focal points for area regeneration initiatives to improve their economic competitiveness. Development should be accommodated in those parts of west London where it will capitalise on its locational advantages and create manufacturing employment opportunities of benefit to London as a whole and to the region.

2.53. Public transport will have a particularly important role to play in west London. The location of many of its key economic areas on major public transport routes should enable development to be less dependent on the use of the car. It will not be appropriate to seek developments which add significantly to the traffic congestion already experienced on the highway network, but it may be appropriate to allow development which requires road freight access and to accept that that may displace car traffic on the grounds that employees should travel by public transport. Special consideration should be given to projects which consolidate planned developments of public transport infrastructure, utilise existing links in the public transport network where capacity is underused or which stimulate potential new public transport opportunities and interchanges.

2.54. The strategic road pattern in west London is already well established. Road access issues predominantly need to tackle local access and congestion, linking the development areas more efficiently to the trunk network and reducing conflict with surrounding residential areas. Public transport improvements focus on the creation of better linkages between the key areas and their surrounding hinterland, and on opportunities for interchange. An example is the development of Willesden Junction as a transport hub, including rapid bus links direct from there into Park Royal. CrossRail, together with improving links to Heathrow, would tie the area in more closely to the economy of both Heathrow and central London. Rail services at present lightly used, could be developed to serve the corridors, particularly through Hayes and Brentford, assisted by programmed electrification and resignalling, improvements to the West London Line and the possibility of new stations and improved interchange facilities at Willesden. The West London Line serves the important exhibition centres of Olympia and Earls Court and better public transport would improve their attractiveness. The other main centre of attraction at Wembley Stadium/Conference Centre already enjoys good public transport access, which London Underground Ltd have developed plans to enhance; thereby improving the site's ability to attract high volumes of participants and spectators to major events in competition with other centres in the UK and Europe.

2.55. An important Borough initiative to foster more sustainable means of transport while encouraging economic growth is SWELTRAC (the South West London Transport Conference). This brings together Boroughs and public transport operators to examine access to Heathrow and to town centres in south and west London. The emphasis is on increasing accessibility by public transport and on restraining car use to ameliorate the existing high levels of congestion. An integrated and coordinated programme of rail, bus priority and traffic management measures is being proposed, linked to economic objectives for the main town centres. In addition, BAA have completed a range of studies into options for improved rail services to Heathrow airport from a variety of destinations. A number of rail, bus and coach links are in prospect, which could also include better connections to Stockley Park, Bedfont Lakes and Feltham.

2.56. In parallel with these initiatives the Department of Transport is conducting a study into service access to London's airports, including Heathrow (the London Airports Surface Access Study (LASAS)). The objectives are to encourage movement towards greater use of public transport to access airports, and to promote alternative modes for both passengers and staff. LASAS is reviewing a range of schemes for access to airports, including those proposed by SWELTRAC and by BAA. Interchange between modes will be important. A report will be completed in 1996. Boroughs should ensure that any schemes arising from the study are promptly incorporated into plans, any necessary safeguarding enforced and that developments are sited to support and benefit from public transport services.

2.57. In common with the other main corridors of London, new partnerships have been established to coordinate area management at the strategic and local level. Harlesden City Challenge is well established, focusing on one of west London's most serious pockets of deprivation. Partnerships at Park Royal, Brentford, Wembley Park, Hayes/West Drayton and Earls Court have also received backing from the SRB. Where these partnerships are split between Boroughs, Boroughs should cooperate to ensure consistency in the reviews of the relevant UDPs. This is particularly important in Park Royal which is split between three Boroughs.

The Wandle Valley

2.58. The Wandle Valley stretches from Wandsworth Riverside to Croydon, linking a series of town centres, older industrial areas and large scale opportunity sites. It also contains a significant number of south London's pockets of deprivation. The main focal points for regeneration include Wandsworth Riverside, where there are currently a number of large vacant riverside sites offering longer term mixed use development opportunities, and the established industrial and manufacturing areas of Mitcham/Beddington and Purley Way, which require restructuring and improvement to sustain their competitiveness, and which contain a number of site development opportunities for employment uses.

2.59. The area has inherited a network of rail based transport although this is not as well focused in the public mind as the Underground north of the river and frequencies are typically lower. The development of Croydon Tramlink would allow a much clearer focus on the important office and town centre of Croydon, together with a modern link to Wimbledon, replacing the rail branch line. Opportunities for further links and interchanges will be created especially arising from the SWELTRAC initiative, which offer the prospect of better access to Heathrow, while good interchanges could allow very high accessibility to central London and Gatwick. Interchange with the proposed Chelsea Hackney Line and the development of Thameslink 2000 would also improve the area's accessibility and viability.

2.60. Development should be planned to improve access from the regional rail network and to the valley's residential hinterland. Other issues that need to be tackled are local road access to industrial sites and town centres, the improvement of environmental quality, especially near the river Wandle, and the enhancement of Metropolitan Open Land. The balance between these issues at the different locations should be articulated in the relevant UDPs.

2.61. The Wandle Valley Partnership, embracing the Boroughs of Wandsworth, Merton, Sutton and Croydon, should continue to work together to implement a planning and regeneration framework for the area. Local partnerships have been established in each of the Wandle Valley Boroughs to promote the economic, social and physical regeneration of the area. The partnerships' efforts are being supported through the SRB in Wandsworth town centre, Merton's industrial estates and Abbey Ward, Sutton's Northern Wards and Roundshaw Estate, and in the South Wandle area of Purley Way/Beddington Lane which straddles Croydon and Sutton.

The River Thames and other London waterways

2.62. Draft Strategic Guidance for the Thames is to be published following this guidance. The final version will constitute supplementary guidance for London and supersede the advice here.

2.63. The Thames is one of London's greatest assets. It flows through the heart of the city and has played a vital role in the history of the capital. London developed around the Thames where the river was both accessible to seagoing ships and could be bridged. The Thames has also been a major determinant of the structure and development of London and many important historical buildings are located along its banks. It is also the UK's busiest port and freight traffic through the Port of London is forecast to grow significantly.

2.64. The Thames is still of central importance today. Five main functions can be identified:

- a major river complex

- a setting for development

- an open space and ecological resource

- a transport artery

- a recreational and leisure facility.

These functions and the potential for conflict between them need to be taken into account in setting priorities and framing policies.

2.65. The Government Office for London commissioned the *Thames Strategy* (Government Office for London 1995a) report to examine the Thames from Hampton Court to Greenwich. (Fig 2.4) This report puts forward a strategy plan and design guidelines for riverside development and recommendations for strategic guidance.

2.66. Strategic Guidance for the Thames will set out the Government's planning policies for the river.

These will provide the context for Boroughs to prepare and update their own policies in respect of the Thames. They should lead to an improvement in the status of the river and in the quality of the riverside's urban and natural environment, and help to achieve the true potential of the river for transport and leisure purposes. The character of the Thames alters through different stretches. Therefore, in developing a policy framework Boroughs should aim to achieve a balance between the principles and a combination of policies that are appropriate for each particular stretch of the river.

2.67. The overall objective should be to enhance the status of the Thames, and in particular to:

- improve the quality of the built environment

- conserve and enhance the natural environment

- facilitate the use of the river for transport and recreational purposes.

2.68. The overall principles should be:

Built environment

- to improve the quality of new development and the existing townscape

- to protect and enhance historic buildings, landscapes and views of importance

Natural environment

- to improve the quality and provision of the open space and landscaping along the river

- to conserve and where possible enhance areas of ecological importance

- to discourage encroachment of development into the river

Use of the river

- to encourage the realisation of the transport potential of the river for passengers and freight

- to safeguard essential river-related land uses

- to encourage the use of the river for recreational purposes

Figure 2.4 River Thames Strategy Plan

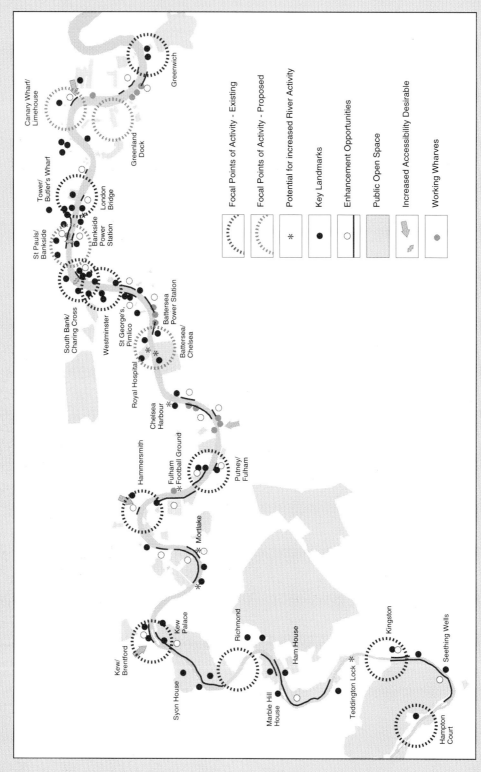

Focal Points of Activity - Existing

Focal Points of Activity - Proposed

Potential for increased River Activity

Key Landmarks

Enhancement Opportunities

Public Open Space

Increased Accessibility Desirable

Working Wharves

Source: 'Thames Strategy: A Study of the Thames prepared for the Government Office for London', Ove Arup Partnership HMSO, 1995.

- to facilitate public access to and along the river.

2.69.   Boroughs should:

- recognise the importance of the Thames and the special considerations that apply to riverside development

- take into account the overall objective and principles for the river

- cooperate with neighbouring authorities and other interests in developing an integrated planning policy framework for the Thames

- through policies and proposals, encourage the maximum use of the river for freight and passenger transport

- safeguard existing river related uses and essential infrastructure.

2.70.   In addition to the Thames, London possesses a wide variety of other waterways including many rivers

and canals (Fig 2.5). Some, such as the River Lee and the Grand Union Canal, are navigable and of metropolitan importance, whilst others are of more local significance. These can contribute greatly to improving the quality of the local environment and quality of life for the people in the area and provide open spaces, a habitat for wildlife, opportunities for leisure and the potential to develop pedestrian and cycle transport routes.

2.71.   Boroughs should recognise the importance of London's waterways and, taking account of the Strategic Guidance for the Thames, include policies for them in their UDPs. In particular Boroughs should:

- seek to improve and enhance the quality and character of London's waterways

- consult with the Environment Agency on the definition of catchment areas for run-off control purposes

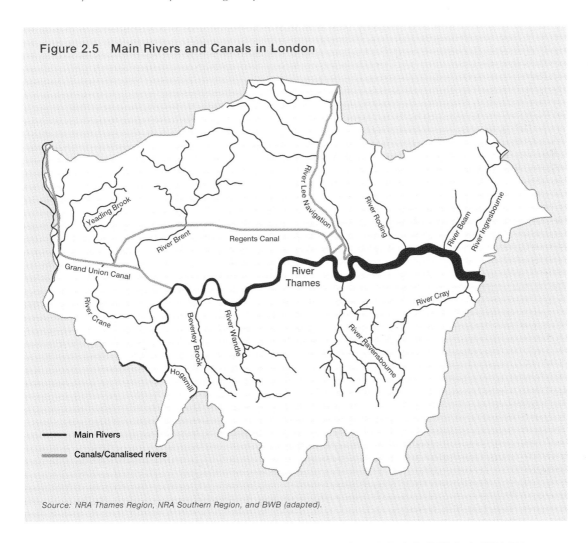

Figure 2.5   Main Rivers and Canals in London

Main Rivers
Canals/Canalised rivers

Source: NRA Thames Region, NRA Southern Region, and BWB (adapted).

- conserve and protect the value of waterways as wildlife habitats

- recognise the potential for recreation and leisure use and develop appropriate proposals to help achieve this potential

- maintain and, where possible, improve access to waterways for pedestrians, cyclists and the disabled.

Map 2   Regeneration in London

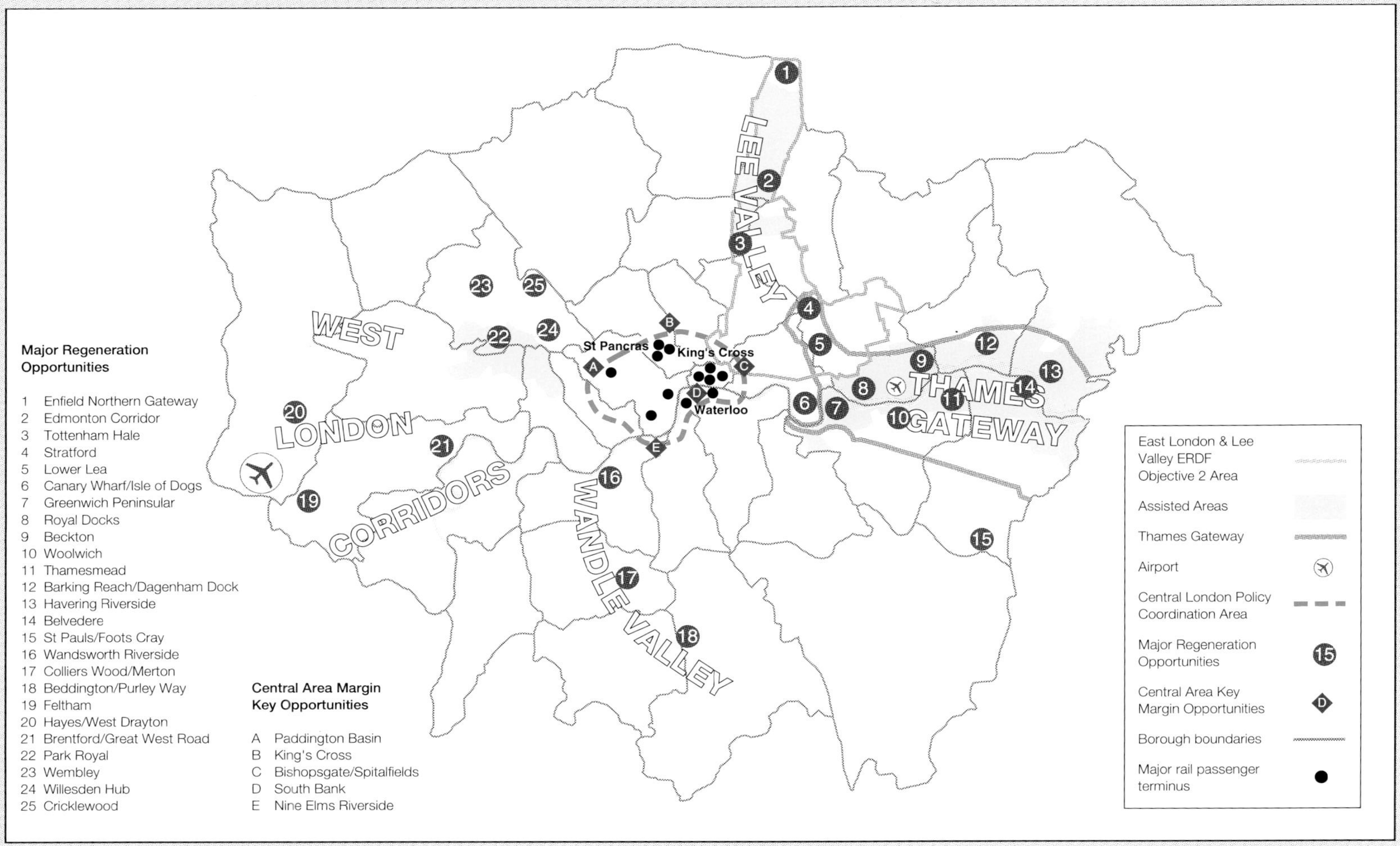

**Major Regeneration
Opportunities**

1   Enfield Northern Gateway
2   Edmonton Corridor
3   Tottenham Hale
4   Stratford
5   Lower Lea
6   Canary Wharf/Isle of Dogs
7   Greenwich Peninsular
8   Royal Docks
9   Beckton
10 Woolwich
11 Thamesmead
12 Barking Reach/Dagenham Dock
13 Havering Riverside
14 Belvedere
15 St Pauls/Foots Cray
16 Wandsworth Riverside
17 Colliers Wood/Merton
18 Beddington/Purley Way
19 Feltham
20 Hayes/West Drayton
21 Brentford/Great West Road
22 Park Royal
23 Wembley
24 Willesden Hub
25 Cricklewood

**Central Area Margin
Key Opportunities**

A   Paddington Basin
B   King's Cross
C   Bishopsgate/Spitalfields
D   South Bank
E   Nine Elms Riverside

Legend:

East London & Lee
Valley ERDF
Objective 2 Area

Assisted Areas

Thames Gateway

Airport

Central London Policy
Coordination Area

Major Regeneration
Opportunities

Central Area Key
Margin Opportunities

Borough boundaries

Major rail passenger
terminus

LEE VALLEY

THAMES GATEWAY

WANDLE VALLEY

WEST LONDON CORRIDORS

St Pancras   King's Cross   Waterloo

Map 3 Central London

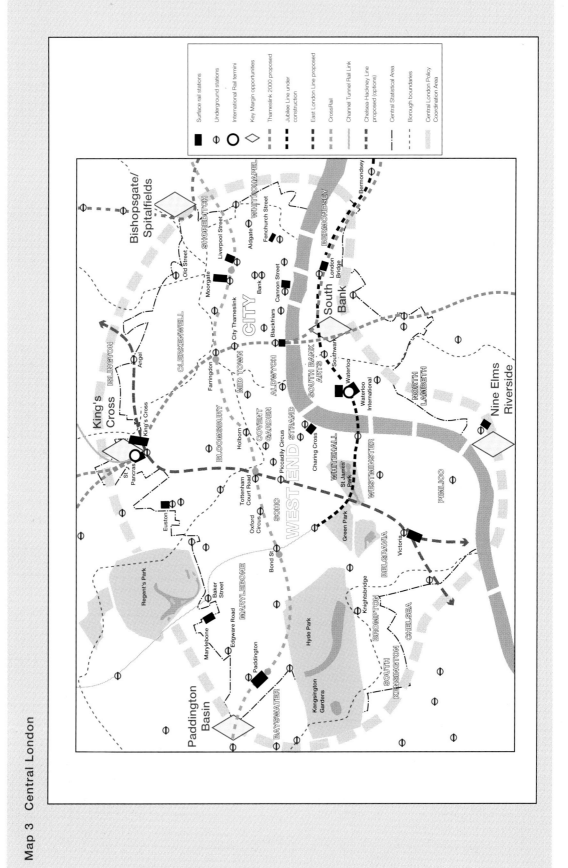

3. London's Economy

Business and Industry

3.1.   London provides jobs for over three million people and a base for nearly a quarter of a million businesses. The Secretary of State has had regard to recent reports which have commented on the recent changes in London's economy, including that prepared for GOL on London in the UK economy and several reports prepared by LPAC, some with a contribution from GOL (Government Office for London 1996a, LPAC 1994b, 1994d, 1994g, 1995e, 1995f). Large cities must expect change as they develop and many of London's strengths and weaknesses are those of many large mature cities. In London, the main changes over recent years include:

- changes in employment including more flexible patterns of working, typified by experiences such as "downsizing" and "outsourcing", leading to a reduction in the numbers of permanent employees at all levels in the workforce. Some processes, including in the service sector, are being automated or have decentralized from London altogether

- a significant increase in output in the financial and business services sectors, enhancing London's position as a world city

- increase in the domination of the local economy by the service sector, which represents over three quarters of output and about 85% of employment

- changes in the demand for and supply of office floorspace, particularly in the Central Area and Docklands, leading to both over supply of space and demand for better quality accommodation

- continued importance of long distance commuting to the Central Area, together with structural imbalance between skills and the labour market, particularly affecting inner London

- decline in some local service industries, partly caused by the decline of London's population (from 8.2 million in 1951 to 6.9 million in 1991), which has affected Boroughs unevenly

- diversification of the local economies of outer London, especially those in the west, with the development of stronger local labour markets and orbital commuting, but with strong competition from towns outside London

- loss of the growth element of many activities to the rest of the country particularly affecting industries which are expected to be of growing economic importance nationally

- decentralisation of activities, following a trend first established as an objective of policy in early post war years, but latterly stimulated by the increased accessibility of outer areas and the rest of the South East (ROSE)

- continued loss of jobs in the manufacturing sector, notably in heavy industry and the concomitant loss of many employment sites to other uses

- changes in geographical organisation and logistics, particularly affected by containerisation and the importance of "just in time" distribution by road, favouring sites on the edge of London and close to new major roads

- the increasing importance of tourism, arts, culture and entertainment both in attracting economic activity to London and in being a source of local employment income

- increasing realisation of the importance of quality of life factors in influencing location decisions.

3.2.   London faces intense competition for development both on international and national levels. Inward investors will weigh up the merits of location in London against other cities. Boroughs should support the efforts being made to support investment in business, commerce and industry. However, London's role in the world economy and in Europe as one of the three world financial centres which each dominate the time zones within which they are situated means that special attention must be given to development which supports the financial and business sectors, together with the facilities which international investors and their employers expect. The primary requirement is therefore to enhance London's role as a world business and commercial centre.

3.3. Boroughs need to develop strategies in partnership with others and in cooperation with each other encouraging economic development and enhancing London's world city status. As well as economic and infrastructure development, London needs environmental improvement. Planning activity should identify the opportunities for wealth creating industries and the environmental features that will attract them and facilitate growth in new businesses. A broader economic base for London will help to secure its long term future and lead to a better prospect for attracting and keeping employment.

3.4. PPG4 sets out national policies relating to the role of industries or business in the planning system. Boroughs should have particular regard to the need to encourage economic activity at all levels in their local economies, and to encourage competitiveness through the provision of attractive and well serviced sites for different types of businesses. ("Business" in this guidance refers to employment generating activities generally and not just to the business use classes in the Use Classes Order (Department of the Environment 1987), unless a specific reference to a particular Use Class is noted. Thus tourism and the arts are both included.)

3.5. The Government wishes to encourage economic development that is compatible with its environmental objectives and which leads to a more effective use of land. Development should improve the environment and contribute to sustainability, especially in regard to transport matters. Businesses, and particularly their main decision makers and employees, have rightly come to recognise that being a bad neighbour creates disbenefits and leads to areas becoming less attractive to economic activity overall. In contrast, the establishment and maintenance of areas of pleasant environment is likely to stimulate further investment.

Performance of the London Economy

Study of London's economy and its linkages with the rest of the UK shows that:
- London has an international competitive advantage in the information and creative industries
- London's economic system extends well beyond its administrative boundaries into the rest of the South East
- long distance commuters from the rest of the South East are important to the economy of the Central Area
- there has been a substantial increase in output in certain sectors, especially in the financial and business services sectors, which produce an output of over £35 billion
- the capital still makes an important contribution to the nation's economy, producing just under 15% of total UK GDP
- London is increasingly dominated by the service sector, which provides 78% of output and 84% of employment
- with the move towards a knowledge based economy, London is well placed to attract businesses and tourism through its strengths in arts, culture and education
- the capital has experienced economic growth without an increase in the number of jobs, partly due to the number of industries and routine office functions which have decentralised away from inner London
- labour markets are very complex but the outer London economies are diversifying, especially those in the west
- inner London has suffered a loss of local employment opportunities, especially through the long term decline of traditional manufacturing activities
- by fostering new and growing firms, London is well placed to attract further investment and activity.

Source: Government Office for London 1996a.

3.6. Boroughs should:

- set out strategic policies in cooperation with neighbouring Boroughs, TECs and business representatives to ensure the right conditions are met to encourage business and industry to locate in, or to remain in, the Borough

- keep under review assessments of the demand and potential demand for industrial and business land in their area. LPAC should provide regular advice on the need for such land in London

- review their policies on the use of land in their area, particularly to assess the scope for identifying land in areas of regeneration which should either be retained or allocated for employment generating uses, or existing sites elsewhere in the Borough which need to be retained for such uses

- promote policies to ensure that jobs and homes are accessible to each other thereby enhancing local employment opportunities, reducing the need to travel and encouraging development in areas served by energy efficient patterns of transport (High trip generating activities should be concentrated in urban and suburban centres.)

- consider the desirability of safeguarding sites for possible specified land uses or mix of uses, in the light of the needs of the industry and business sectors of the local and London wide economy

- consider the needs of visitors to London and promote policies to support tourism by the provision of hotels and services so that London can maximise its tourist potential

- set out policies to create and maintain a good working environment, including minimising pollution and adverse impacts on the locality

- assess the impact of environmental constraints or the likelihood of continued traffic congestion on proposals and seek, where possible, to reduce or mitigate these effects.

Offices

3.7.   Investigation of the office market for LPAC, GOL and the City Corporation (LPAC 1995e) has suggested that there are three major categories of office activity in London:

- organisations serving the international community, including international capital markets, insurance, higher order legal and accountancy firms, broadcasting and media organisations and the headquarters of multinational corporations. This category is showing dynamic growth in output if not necessarily in employment. It requires high quality premises

- employers primarily serving the UK economy, including government, clearing banks, financial and professional services, retailing and transport. These face a difficult future, with pressure for cost cutting, especially in the cost of property. This can lead to decentralisation of all or many activities from London

- companies serving the first two categories and the London economy generally, depending on the vitality of the economy and the need for services which large office based organisations consume. Companies are subject to the effects of recession, but can benefit from changing market conditions, for example cheaper space.

3.8.   All three categories of offices are experiencing pressures to reduce employment. There is generally demand for less space overall, but an expectation that the space occupied should be of higher quality than much of the current office stock. In addition, greater flexibility is being demanded so that occupiers of the larger offices can decide whether to operate in open offices or dealing floors, or in a cellular layout. The net effect is to generate a demand for new high quality offices while releasing more secondary stock on to the market. This trend seems likely to continue, at least in the short to medium term, whilst the influence of changing patterns of work through the application of information technology will need to be monitored.

3.9.   The development of large amounts of office space, mainly in the City of London and Docklands, has led to a very high potential office supply in terms of planning permissions and considerable amounts of underoccupied space and vacant sites. There is therefore a considerable choice for those wishing to occupy or develop office space throughout London varying widely in terms of quality and price. International organisations are expected to seek high quality space and will need to locate close to international transport facilities and the existing critical mass of activity in the Central Area. This suggests that, despite the overall potential over supply, there may be scope for further development in the Central Area or on its margins, close to termini or stations serving international traffic. There is likely to be less scope in the future for office led redevelopment on other sites, while in secondary locations market conditions are likely to suggest a shift away from offices to other land uses.

3.10.   The Secretary of State supports LPAC's proposals to set up an office monitoring panel to report regularly on the state of London's office market. He requests that regular reports are prepared on the different sectors of London's office market to inform investors, developers and planning

Figure 3.1 Major Office and Light Industry (Use Class B1) - Development Floorspace Granted 1989 to 1994

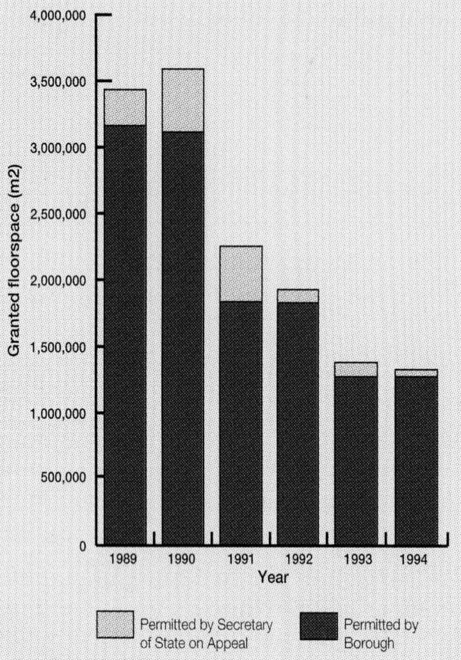

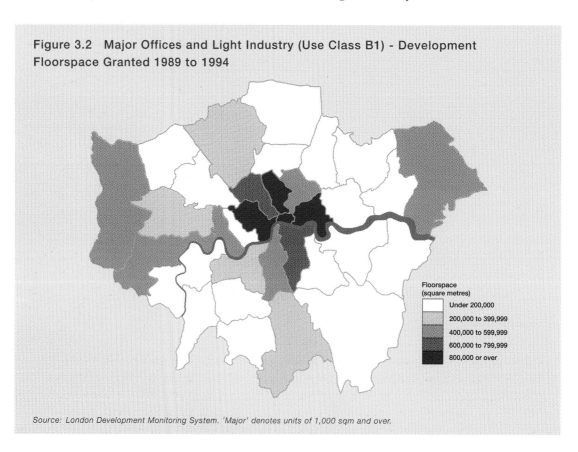

Source: London Development Monitoring System. 'Major' denotes units of 1,000 sqm and over.

authorities of changes in supply and demand and to assist London First in seeking to promote London's sites internationally. Good up to date data is essential if London is to grasp the opportunities and make the best use of its available sites. All participants should strive to make data available to common definitions and standards, but the local authorities could do more to ensure planning is responsive by cooperating in keeping and publishing up to date planning data. Figures 3.1 and 3.2 show relevant data from the London Development Monitoring System.

3.11. Boroughs should:

- take account of up to date information on office stock and development trends and market demands in preparing strategic policies on the role of different locations in their areas for different types of offices

- set out policies for offices, particularly encouraging a range of space to meet different requirements in accessible locations close to public transport facilities

- review proposals for major office development to examine the potential for and desirability of office use against the scope for alternative or mixed uses

Figure 3.2 Major Offices and Light Industry (Use Class B1) - Development Floorspace Granted 1989 to 1994

Source: London Development Monitoring System. 'Major' denotes units of 1,000 sqm and over.

- keep under review areas of existing office development and prepare policies setting out the balance between continued office use and other uses

- prepare policies to enhance the environment within which offices are located, to maintain London's attractiveness to different types of enterprise requiring different sites and layouts

- be flexible, within the requirements of conservation and respect for the heritage, on the changes needed to buildings to meet changing office requirements

- collect and make available up to date data on the planning status of sites, applications, decisions and completions to assist LPAC in monitoring the office market.

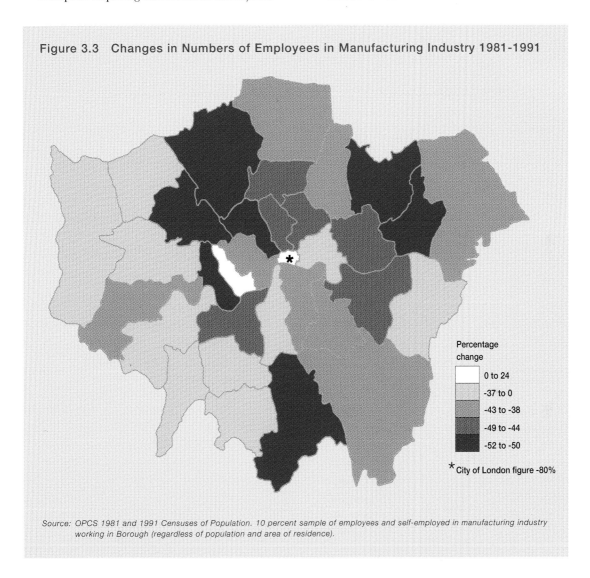

Figure 3.3   Changes in Numbers of Employees in Manufacturing Industry 1981-1991

Percentage change

0 to 24

-37 to 0

-43 to -38

-49 to -44

-52 to -50

* City of London figure -80%

Source: OPCS 1981 and 1991 Censuses of Population. 10 percent sample of employees and self-employed in manufacturing industry working in Borough (regardless of population and area of residence).

Manufacturing and other industry

3.12.   Manufacturing industry in London has been declining in both output and employment terms for many years. Figure 3.3 provides an indication of the change across London. Although part of this can be attributed to greater productivity, it also reflects a relative decline in the importance of industry in the capital. Many sectors of industry in London have lost their share of national GDP in comparison with ROSE and the rest of the UK. London needs to become more attractive to industry, especially to

provide locations for the manufacture of technologically based high value goods which show good prospects for national growth. Boroughs should actively seek to redress the trend whereby London's share of "high tech" employment appears to have fallen in recent years.

3.13.   As part of the programme of activity following the White Papers on Competitiveness (HM Government 1994b, 1995a), the Government will be working with London's manufacturers to identify ways in which the sector can be rejuvenated.

Boroughs have a vital role to play in identifying sites and facilitating development for companies that wish to locate or expand in their areas. Borough planning and economic development departments should work closely together with TECs and with other agencies to encourage manufacturing. However, it is not the availability of land that is necessarily the key to meeting the needs of industry. There is a considerable amount of under used land, but quality, location and site conditions are frequently very important. There should therefore be a consistent attempt to improve the environmental quality of the areas surrounding them, their access, particularly for goods vehicles, and in the facilities offered to those who could be attracted to work in them.

Manufacturing in London

Manufacturing activity has declined significantly in recent years. In the early 1980s manufacturing accounted for 17% of London's GDP compared to 13% in 1993. In employment terms about 19% of London's workforce were employed in manufacturing in the early 1980s as against 9% now.

The Government believes that an active and thriving manufacturing sector is vital to the success of London's economy. It is committed to the revival of manufacturing in London and is taking the following action:

- working with industry, local authorities, TECs and other partners to define and facilitate local action programmes to support manufacturing
- through the London First Centre, targeting foreign manufacturing companies, especially "high tech" companies, to locate in London
- assisting in the improvement of industry's image and encouraging environmental awareness - modern manufacturing facilities should be regarded as a benefit to an area
- improving the information base on London's manufacturing sector.

3.14. PPG4 sets out further guidance, including the requirement that a variety of sites should be made available to meet differing needs. In London there will be scope to encourage development for a range of enterprises and to improve the vitality of manufacturing. In particular, it should be possible to capitalize on the economic linkages between the most successful sectors of the capital's economy and the activities needed to support it. Industries such as printing, transport and communications are vital to the functioning of world city activities and greater effort should be made to secure them in London.

3.15. Where there is no prospect for the development of existing land currently allocated for industrial use, land should be brought into other beneficial uses, including housing development or mixed use schemes. However, this should not occur without there being a clear assessment of the value of retaining the land for industrial or business uses, together with an appreciation of the employment effects of different solutions. Figure 3.4 indicates the distribution of the permissions granted over recent years for general industrial (B2) development of over 1000 m^2 gross floorspace.

3.16. Sites can be divided into three categories:

- industrial medium to large scale sites which should meet the needs of most B2 uses in the Use Classes Order, and in some cases B8, because of their access (especially for freight movements), layout, landscaping and cost requirements

- industrial and business sites, meeting the needs of B1 (b) and B1 (c) activities, requiring a high quality environment and less access for heavy goods vehicles but which should have good accessibility by public transport and relate more harmoniously with neighbouring uses than B2 or B8

- "Technoparks", where a very high quality environment can be established or maintained and where links between business and research can be enhanced or fostered. They may, according to type, density of development and scale, be either in campus or urban locations but should be very accessible by public transport.

3.17. LPAC has considered sites which appear to offer the best prospects for development for major employment generating uses. Figure 3.5 shows LPAC's Preferred Industrial Locations and Business Parks which relate respectively to the first two site

Figure 3.4 Permissions for Major General Industrial Development (Use Class B2) by Size, Granted 1989 to 1994

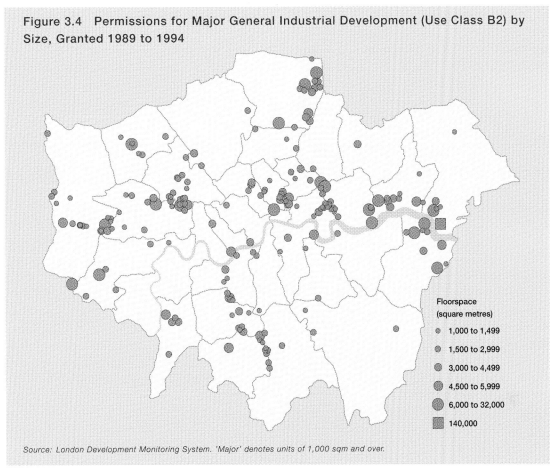

Floorspace
(square metres)

○ 1,000 to 1,499
◎ 1,500 to 2,999
● 3,000 to 4,499
● 4,500 to 5,999
● 6,000 to 32,000
■ 140,000

Source: London Development Monitoring System. 'Major' denotes units of 1,000 sqm and over.

Figure 3.5 LPAC's Preferred Strategic Employment Sites

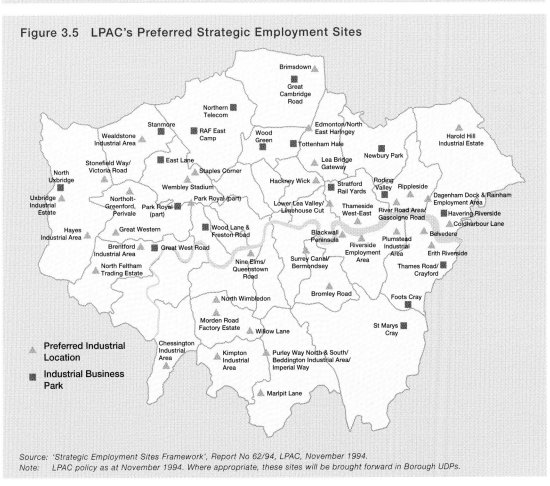

△ Preferred Industrial
   Location

■ Industrial Business
   Park

Source: 'Strategic Employment Sites Framework', Report No 62/94, LPAC, November 1994.
Note: LPAC policy as at November 1994. Where appropriate, these sites will be brought forward in Borough UDPs.

categories described above. These sites should be especially considered when planning or regenerating activities are contemplated and preference be given for retaining them for employment uses, although a degree of mixed used development may be appropriate. Many more industries occupy sites which are integral to their local economy but which are vulnerable to development proposals from higher value uses. Boroughs may seek to safeguard such sites by restricting prospective land uses to those offering employment in industry and business classes. However, the case should be well justified on the basis of the contribution that employment on or associated with these sites makes to the economy of the Borough and of London as a whole and that there continues to be a reasonable prospect of productive use. The conversion of sites currently dependant on road access to more general office uses attracting car commuters or retailing attracting car borne shoppers should be resisted.

3.18. It will not normally be acceptable for Boroughs to propose policies restricting the operation of the B1 use class. However, such policies may be appropriate in exceptional clearly defined locations where the authority is able to demonstrate that flexibility causes significant difficulties when trying to protect existing or proposed industrial and mixed use areas. Such action might be appropriate for:

- sites to be developed as "Technoparks" (Table 3.1), where preference should be given to the B1 (b) use class or for specified high technology uses. This will often best take place in conjunction with a management strategy for the technopark, including the negotiation of s106 Obligations

- sites which can be shown to have unique qualities, for example in terms of location, access or layout, suggesting that they should be available for manufacturing industry well into the future

- site which should be safeguarded on grounds of access, particularly close to rail lines where rail freight facilities can be arranged, or on the Thames and other waterways, where water transport is possible

- areas containing specialist and often small industries which contribute to local and London economic life and have significant environmental characteristics but which are in danger of being squeezed out by more general commercial development

- areas which are developing around arts, cultural or entertainment facilities where too great a concentration of office uses may inhibit the mixed use character of the area. Where a distinctive

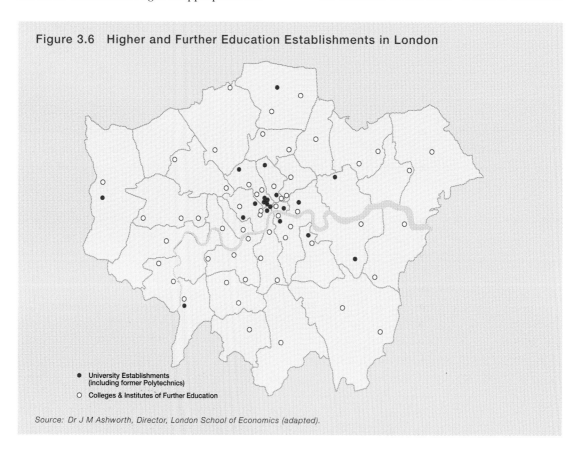

Figure 3.6   Higher and Further Education Establishments in London

● University Establishments
  (including former Polytechnics)
○ Colleges & Institutes of Further Education

Source: Dr J M Ashworth, Director, London School of Economics (adapted).

sense of place can be defined, it would be appropriate to safeguard these by use of policies applying to a defined area based on the current extent of the artistic quarter.

Where sites or areas are to be safeguarded by policies in the plan, they should be clearly identified on the Proposals Map and be well justified.

3.19. The existence in London of world class educational and medical establishments, together with the headquarters offices of many firms and departments of state, suggest that London should be well placed to secure enterprise at the forefront of technology. Figure 3.6 shows the distribution of higher and further education establishments across London. London is, however, poorly represented and has no "technopark" or "science park" of the scale of, for example, Cambridge or Aston (West Midlands). A recent study for LPAC and GOL (LPAC 1995f) concluded that there were only two small established schemes in London, compared to 43 elsewhere in the country.

Table 3.1 Possible Types of Technoparks for London

Technoparks can be developed in a variety of ways but it may be convenient to describe them in relation to four types:

- **large scale strategic locations (often over 20 hectares) with high quality premises typically linked to a prestigious university. Services are geared to the needs of large firms, but many of the users may be relatively independent**
- **smaller science and technology parks, attracting mainly small local firms on sites between 2 to 20 hectares, and related to an institution with a good reputation for links with local business and industries. Good local management and site availability provides support for firms which might otherwise move out of the area**
- **incubator or innovation centres, developed on a small scale to provide reasonable priced accommodation on flexible terms to new start-up and small local firms. Management is active in providing supporting services to the occupants and there may be close links with universities, sometimes sharing the image of the university in terms of site quality. They are particularly suitable in high density locations**
- **networks, where links develop between sites and parks, local universities or other institutions, and the local economy. Having a less physical manifestation, networks are often complementary to the other three types.**

Source: LPAC 1995f.

3.20. The study estimated that London needs at least 200,000 m^2 floorspace for technology parks up to 2001. Although there are several schemes in an advanced state, their geographical distribution tends to reflect the availability of sites having regard to established developers' criteria (as for more general business parks). There is an opportunity to develop sites in closer physical proximity of the institutions with which they might be linked, which suggests a concerted effort to find more sites and premises in inner London, closer to the major institutions, and where their location will benefit the local economy. There is also scope to support clusters of firms in sectors, such as multi media, printing and fashion, through policies which encourage the formation of businesses and the use of business premises in existing built up areas.

3.21. Boroughs should:

- review the extent of industrial land in their Borough, having regard to current trends in employment and to the sites identified by LPAC (Fig 3.5) and make strategic policies for the furtherance of industry and manufacturing

- consider the scope for the development of technoparks and, where appropriate, identify sites, having regard to likely linkages with universities, medical establishments or other institutions and the availability of public transport

- prepare policies to ensure that the most important employment sites are safeguarded from other uses where this can be clearly justified

- identify and clearly justify those areas where restrictions should apply to the B1 use class, or where preference should be given to defined uses as part of mixed use schemes.

Distribution, warehousing and freight handling

3.22. Distribution and warehousing should be important components of a large metropolitan area. The development of sites to serve London will be an important complement to manufacturing activity. Regeneration activity in the main London corridors can also be expected to increase demand for these activities. However, London faces fierce competition from the rest of the South East. Opportunities exist in part of London, particularly in the east, in the Thames Gateway and in the regeneration corridors, where land availability and improvements in accessibility will provide potential locations capable of serving regional, national and European markets. Sites identified by LPAC (Fig 3.5) may be particularly suitable for distribution. Figure 3.7 shows the distribution of major storage and distribution (B8) developments granted across London in recent years.

3.23. There are good opportunities for the movement of heavy flows of freight by rail or water.

It is important to encourage more freight movement by these modes, especially given the opportunities provided by the opening of the Channel Tunnel and the benefits of the Single European Market. Grants are available under sections 139 and 140 of the 1993 Railways Act to encourage the removal of heavy lorries from the road network by assisting companies to invest in rail or inland waterway facilities. Reviews of UDPs should be the opportunity for a renewed consideration of the potential for rail or water based sites, in cooperation with operators, the Port of London Authority (PLA) and Railtrack. There is scope for the use of waterside sites throughout the Thames in London. In particular the Thames Gateway Planning Framework explains how the potential of the lower Thames can be realised and seeks to avoid the loss of the waterfront to developments which do not benefit functionally from a riverside location.

3.24. Boroughs should:

• promote positive policies for distribution, warehousing and freight movement, including

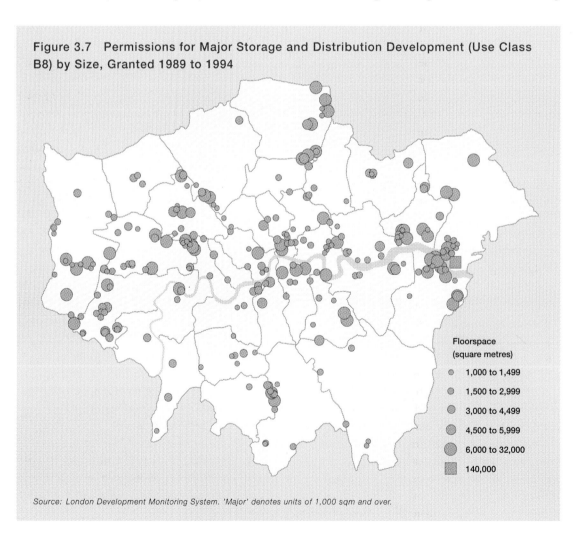

Figure 3.7 Permissions for Major Storage and Distribution Development (Use Class B8) by Size, Granted 1989 to 1994

Floorspace
(square metres)

○ 1,000 to 1,499

◉ 1,500 to 2,999

● 3,000 to 4,499

● 4,500 to 5,999

● 6,000 to 32,000

■ 140,000

Source: London Development Monitoring System. 'Major' denotes units of 1,000 sqm and over.

identifying sites and assisting in making land available

- identify the opportunities for freight handling and transfer by rail or water and safeguard sites where there is a reasonable prospect of freight being transported by these modes.

Arts, culture and entertainment

3.25.   These activities contribute significantly to the life and attractiveness of London as well as being important employers of labour in their own right. They encompass several activities ranging from the performing arts to recording media, from visual arts to multi media development, and have strong links with education, museums, design, fashion and the graphic arts. The premises that they occupy therefore may involve several different land uses. There is also likely to be more flexibility in their location and use of space in the future, reflecting the impact of new technology.

3.26.   London already exhibits a critical mass in the creative activities and it is the one major employment sector which has demonstrated positive employment growth in recent years relative to the rest of the UK. It is therefore vital that these activities are supported by a positive approach from planning authorities. Although potentially a footloose collection of activities - and some aspects, for example production on location, will always be dispersed - there are benefits for the industry of face to face contact and the cross-fertilisation of ideas. Many activities are likely to continue to concentrate in parts of the Central Area, close to established cultural and entertainment facilities. A thriving local arts environment can also lead to the development of cultural quarters, which in turn can become the focus of visitor attraction programmes and hotel development. There is considerable scope to encourage such quarters to assist this sector to grow and to contribute to the regeneration of parts of inner London.

3.27.   Many of the measures to be taken to assist this sector will be to improve the quality of the environment generally and to facilitate linkages between the different players. Particularly in emerging cultural quarters, Boroughs need to demonstrate flexibility in dealing with applications, especially where mixed uses would be beneficial. There are considerable opportunities for arts related activities to be located in and around town centres

but out of centre car dependent leisure and entertainment facilities should be discouraged.

3.28.   Boroughs should:

- identify areas which demonstrate a concentration of arts, culture and entertainment activities when reviewing plans

- prepare policies to support the activities of this sector, particularly in and around the Central Area and in town centres

- ensure that policies to improve the built and open environment assist in providing the quality of environment which is needed to underpin the activities of this sector.

Hotels, conferences and exhibitions

3.29.   Tourism is one of London's growth sectors and it will be vital to the future success of the capital's economy that opportunities are embraced. Measures to improve the quality of London's environment and its transport systems will assist in making London more attractive to visitors, as well as encouraging a more positive approach to the enhancement of tourist sites and the development of visitor facilities.

3.30.   The London Tourist Board (LTB) has developed a hotel development initiative to encourage investment in hotel accommodation and other tourist facilities, especially on the edge of the Central Area. Current visitor projections indicate that London faces an acute shortage of medium-priced bedspace and that the market could readily absorb an additional 10,000 rooms by 2000. Such a shortage poses a serious threat to the growth potential of the sector and Boroughs should respond by identifying suitable sites close to attractions and public transport. Figure 3.8 shows the distribution over recent years of hotel developments of 10 beds or more.

3.31.   There is now considerable scope to develop hotels in parts of London which will add to capacity and assist the local economy by providing opportunities for service employment, other local services and the development of visitor attractions. The main considerations are:

- hotels should be located close to public transport facilities providing accessibility to international and national transport termini and the Central Area

Figure 3.8 Permissions for Major Hotel Developments (Use Class C1) by Size, Granted 1989 to 1994

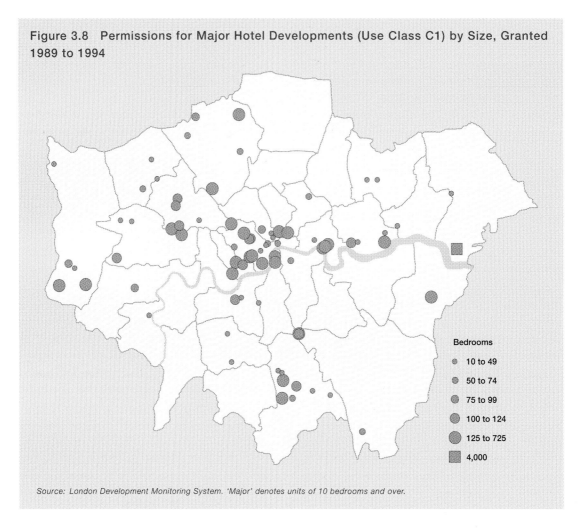

Bedrooms

- ⦁ 10 to 49
- ⦁ 50 to 74
- ● 75 to 99
- ● 100 to 124
- ● 125 to 725
- ■ 4,000

Source: London Development Monitoring System. 'Major' denotes units of 10 bedrooms and over.

- the provision of picking up and setting down facilities for coaches and taxis will need to be considered in decisions on the location and design of hotels

- over-concentration of hotels in limited areas in the Central Area should be avoided but there exists scope to develop some vacant office space for hotels in parts of the Central Area

- sites on the edge of the Central Area will be suitable for hotels if they are accessible, contribute to the regeneration of these areas and if development respects neighbouring residential communities

- town centres throughout London are suitable locations for additional hotels, especially those near to major visitor attractions.

3.32. Boroughs should not seek to restrict hotel development throughout their area. In a very few areas the extreme concentration of hotels could displace other uses, particularly residential accommodation, and reduce the effective catchment of community facilities, for example local shops and schools. Where this seems likely to cause demonstrable harm, Boroughs could prepare policies restricting hotels in clearly defined areas by giving preference to established uses, but only where this is exceptionally well justified. In some areas of current excess supply of lower price hotels, encouragement could be given to upgrading to create better quality stock.

3.33. London is important for both conference facilities and exhibition centres, but such activities need continuing investment to compete with facilities elsewhere. Considerable investment has taken place elsewhere in Europe and exhibitions are becoming more international in scope. Clearly there are only limited opportunities for new major centres attracting the highest volumes of visitors but scope exists for the improvement of existing facilities and for more regionally based conference facilities. Careful consideration will need to be given to parking and accessibility and the relationship with neighbouring areas, but the largest and most popular centres may demonstrate a need for expansion which should be encouraged if strategic planning policies are not compromised (for example Green Belt or Metropolitan Open Land). Opportunities for developing public transport services should be taken to minimise traffic congestion, nuisance and the use of land for parking, and to maximise the number of visitors and staff using sustainable means of transport.

3.34. Boroughs should:

- consider the need for hotel development for different price ranges in their Boroughs, having regard to the LTB's information on the supply of and demand for hotel spaces

- prepare policies to encourage hotels in areas that would be acceptable for visitors, benefit the local economy and be accessible to public transport

- consider the use of existing vacant space (including office uses and sites in the Central Area margins and in town centres) for hotels, and make proposals accordingly

- include policies and proposals for major conference and exhibition facilities, the improvement of existing facilities and the development of new sites where this is appropriate.

4. Housing

4.1.   London's supply of land is limited, leading to an imbalance between housing supply and demand. The establishment of the Green Belt put an end to the continuous physical spread of London, while for many years an objective of policy was to reduce the very high densities of some inner areas. London's post war population declined until recently (Fig 4.1) but the number of households has increased due to a significant rise in the numbers of one and two person households. OPCS population projections indicate the potential for a significant increase in London's population up to 2011 and projections suggest a proportionately greater increase in the number of households (Department of the Environment 1995e) (Fig 4.2). Boroughs should seek to make the maximum contribution to meeting the demands for housing in London and to encourage the provision of well designed housing of all types whilst safeguarding the quality of the environment. This will contribute to the implementation of policies for the more efficient use of urban land, the conservation of the Green Belt and the principles of sustainable development.

4.2.   The Government has indicated its commitment to addressing the national context for the future of housing in the White Paper *Our Future Homes* (HM Government 1995b). This stresses the important role that planning has in providing new homes. Boroughs should have specific regard as to how their UDPs, together with their associated housing strategies and regeneration proposals, are promoting policies and proposals which address the key national targets set for 2005 to enable everyone to have a choice of decent housing.

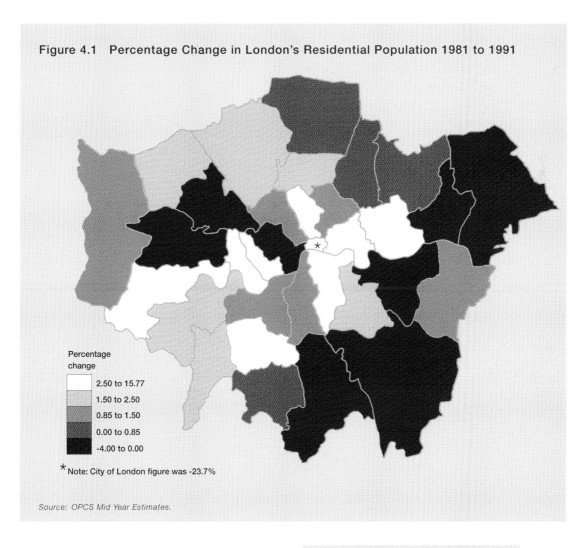

Figure 4.1   Percentage Change in London's Residential Population 1981 to 1991

Percentage change

2.50 to 15.77
1.50 to 2.50
0.85 to 1.50
0.00 to 0.85
-4.00 to 0.00

* Note: City of London figure was -23.7%

Source: OPCS Mid Year Estimates.

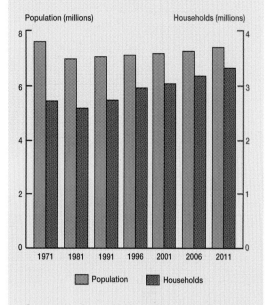

Figure 4.2 Projected Population and Household Formation 1971 to 2011

Population (millions)   Households (millions)

Population   Households

Source: 1991 Census OPCS, and DoE.
Note: The population and household projections for
         1996 and onwards indicate what would happen if
         past trends were to continue; they are not policy
         based forecasts of what the Government expects
         or intends to happen.

Targets for the Next Decade

Enable everyone to have a choice of decent housing

Key national targets by 2005:

- **Increase the number of owner occupied homes by 1.5 million**
- **Reduce significantly the proportion of homes lying empty to 3%**
- **Build half of all new homes on re-used sites**
- **Transform, through a public and private sector partnership, the remaining large scale poor quality public estates**
- **Ensure that there is no necessity for people to sleep rough.**

Source: HM Government 1995b.

The regional context

4.3. London must be viewed in its regional context. Regional Guidance for the South East (RPG 9) refers to the change in household composition, the complex pattern of migration in the region and the pattern of new dwelling provision in the South East. London's total population is related more to its

supply of dwellings, rather than to the total level of housing demand. The fact that there is - and is likely to remain - an excess of demand over supply in London leads to a need to consider carefully the provision of all housing, including that for affordable and special needs.

4.4. RPG9 sets out the regional rate of provision of 57,000 net additional dwellings per annum from 1991 to 2006. The London component on this basis is 17,333 p.a.. These figures take into account the 1989-based population and household projections. Updated 1992 - based sub-national population and household projections were published in 1994 and 1995 respectively (Fig 4.2). The implications of these later projections will be considered during the review of RPG9 but revised regional figures will not be prepared until after the publication of this Strategic Guidance. In the meantime, this Guidance accepts the current RPG9 figure as the continuing strategic objective for London. This is because the London dwelling provision is based on London's ability to provide dwellings within a broad assumption of the continuation of current policies and densities, rather than to meet any specified level of demand. The dwelling provision will continue to be informed by population and household forecasts but will not be constrained or led by them. In considering the figures to which Borough UDPs should aspire, this Guidance has had regard to national and regional policy, studies of housing supply made by LPAC's *London's Housing Capacity* (LPAC 1994e) and the achievement of Boroughs in granting planning permission affecting housing since the publication of the first RPG3. The overall number of dwellings, in developments of 10 or more dwellings, granted planning permission between 1989 and 1994 is shown in Figure 4.3. Further guidance on monitoring is given in Chapter 10.

The net additional housing provision

4.5. The first Strategic Guidance for London indicated a provision of 260,000 additional dwellings for the period 1987 - 2001. It also allowed Boroughs to apply a general presumption against the loss of housing to other uses. These levels of provision have been tested in individual Borough UDPs, with the result that London has been found to be able to make a significant contribution to meeting its demands for housing. According to a LPAC survey (LPAC 1994j), in the first five years of this period 146,273 dwellings were approved and 105,792 completed.

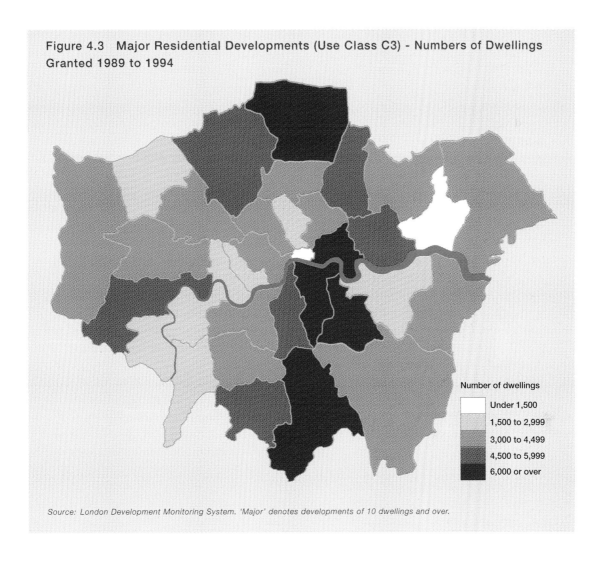

Figure 4.3   Major Residential Developments (Use Class C3) - Numbers of Dwellings
Granted 1989 to 1994

Number of dwellings

Under 1,500

1,500 to 2,999

3,000 to 4,499

4,500 to 5,999

6,000 or over

Source: London Development Monitoring System. 'Major' denotes developments of 10 dwellings and over.

4.6.   The contribution which can be made to achieving additional dwellings is broadly made up of four components:

• new dwellings provided on sites redeveloped or made available from other uses, including a housing component in suitable mixed use development

• the adaptation of existing buildings in other uses for housing

• the redevelopment of land used for housing to a higher density

• the conversion of the existing housing stock for occupation by more households.

The balance between these will vary according to location, market demands and housing need. It is likely that "windfall" sites will continue to make some contribution in many areas. Boroughs should consider allocating for housing sites which are currently vacant or under used, including a new or increased provision of housing in mixed use schemes. Recent research (London Research Centre et al 1992.) has shown a substantial stock of property which has the potential to be converted to provide additional housing units. Work undertaken for LPAC and others (LPAC 1994c) suggests that the conversion of offices to housing would also be a beneficial use of currently under-used assets in some areas. Such change of use should be encouraged to introduce mixed uses into town centres and increase their vitality, as well as the use of premises over shops for residential use.

4.7.   LPAC's 1994 Advice was that an optimal provision of housing to 2006 would be 234,000 net additional dwellings, with an additional contribution possible from the conversion of vacant office space to residential use. Boroughs accepted this figure on the basis of current policies, standards and market conditions. Whilst accepting the estimates of capacity as being a fair appraisal of the implications of current conditions and policies, the Secretary of State does not consider that they provide a sufficient forward looking basis for Boroughs planning for the next round of UDPs. In particular, the LPAC Advice assumed a continuing depressed market for conversions, the use of more restrictive standards to be applied within UDPs, and in some cases the requirement for minimum off street car parking provision. These assumptions may have unduly limited the potential gains to the housing stock that could result from increased conversion activity which can be achieved without reducing the quality of the urban environment. The Secretary of State found it necessary to object to a number of policies in the first round UDPs which sought to impose development control standards in a prescriptive manner. Given the continuing need for housing within London and the overall age of the stock, Boroughs need to consider the implications of the changing composition of the population, whilst having continuing and proper regard to the amenity of residential areas (discussed in Chapter 8).

4.8.   Table 4.1 presents the additional net dwellings as proposed by LPAC in 1994 Advice. In the light of the need to have regard to the principles of sustainable development, to ensure that as many as possible of London's residents and workers are housed within the capital, and to respond to the continuing demand for housing as demonstrated in successive population and household projections, the figures in the table should be regarded as the minimum net additional completions over the period to be proposed within the UDP and tested against the policies of this Guidance in further UDP inquiries.

4.9.   Each Borough will need to demonstrate in its review of the UDP that it has had regard to the requirement to provide the maximum number of dwellings, subject to the maintenance of a quality environment, and to show what additional housing can be provided above the figures in the table during the remaining years of this Guidance. Policies and proposals to maximise the dwelling provision should be prepared and tested at future public inquiries into the alteration or replacement of UDPs and justified in respect of the four components listed in paragraph 4.6. The effects of different standards for parking and for amenity space and layout should be made explicit.

4.10.   Boroughs should have regard to the objectives of national guidance on housing land supply given in PPG3. However, in view of the complex factors affecting land availability for housing in London, the requirement in the national guidance to identify a five-year supply of sites for housing does not apply. In reviewing UDPs, account should be taken of the need for and, the ability to provide for, a range of housing types, from single persons' units and units for small households to family accommodation, including housing suitable for larger families.

4.11.   Boroughs should:

- set out strategic policies for increasing housing provision in their area, having regard to the need to contribute to the regional housing provision

- demonstrate how they have assessed the demand and potential supply of different types of housing, to meet different household sizes in the light of demographic characteristics and trends

- show how they propose to exceed the minimum figures set down in Table 4.1 for net additional dwelling completions up to 2006

- identify the contribution housing can make on vacant or under-used sites

- identify the scope for housing as part of mixed use schemes.

Reuse and conversion of existing stock

4.12.   If Boroughs are to provide for a higher dwelling provision than that indicated in the LPAC Advice whilst adequately safeguarding the quality of the environment, it will be necessary for a fresh approach to be taken towards the identification of new housing opportunities, both from possible new sites and from new conversions from non-traditional sources such as obsolete office floorspace. The renewal of run down areas provides scope to improve the local environment, and positive action through investment in the urban fabric instills confidence within local communities. There is also scope, through conversions, to increase the provision of dwellings for a growing number of small households.

4.13.   Surplus office floorspace is a potential major source of such new housing. Depending on the view taken of the prospects for new offices and the continued direction and scale of change in clerical employment, it is estimated by LPAC that there could be scope for over 30,000 dwellings as a result of conversions from offices. Market conditions and developer interest suggest that a growing contribution could be made, given positive planning policies from Boroughs. A variety of approaches will need to be considered if this potential is to be realised. Some offices in suburban locations could lend themselves to residential uses, perhaps improving the mix of dwelling sizes in the neighbourhood. Other sites are on the fringe of the Central Area and in town centres throughout London. Conversions can contribute to bringing life and stability to areas in which population has declined in the past. It will also support local economic activity especially the viability of services to the local population, and may assist in reducing travel needs, thereby contributing to sustainability.

Table 4.1 LPAC's Advice on Dwelling Provision (1992-2006) by Borough

Borough	Additional Dwellings
City of London	120
Barking and Dagenham	7000
Barnet	10,800
Bexley	5,450
Brent	6,850
Bromley	8,650
Camden	9,700
Croydon	9,700
Ealing	8,100
Enfield	10,600
Greenwich	10,750
Hackney	5,850
Hammersmith and Fulham	4,950
Haringey	6,700
Harrow	3,180
Havering	5,550
Hillingdon	3,900
Hounslow	6,100
Islington	5,750
Kensington and Chelsea	7,750
Kingston-upon-Thames	4,250
Lambeth	7,700
Lewisham	8,400
Merton	5,000
Newham	8,300
Redbridge	10,800
Richmond-upon-Thames	4,550
Southwark	10,300
Sutton	5,400
Tower Hamlets	10,650
Waltham Forest	4,950
Wandsworth	7,700
Westminster	8,650
TOTAL	234,100

Source: LPAC 1994a.
Note: Figures for individual Boroughs rounded to the nearest 10.

4.14. Further opportunities include sites not currently identified for residential development but on which other uses are unlikely to come forward. They may include the re-use, change of use or conversion of vacant buildings, sites with unimplemented planning permissions and the potential from vacant premises above shops and mixed use schemes. Such conversions and changes of use should be encouraged and facilitated through planning policies.

4.15. Conversions of existing residential properties to two or more units have traditionally provided an important contribution to the increase in London's housing stock. However, such activity has recently tended to decrease, and LPAC's study, *London's Housing Capacity* (LPAC 1994e) assumes that it will remain low. There remains, however, scope for conversions in suitable locations, and it should be an aim of planning in London to identify such locations and, where appropriate, to increase such activity during the period covered by this Guidance.

4.16. Enabling a more effective use of housing land and seeking housing in areas of mixed uses will make a significant contribution to achieving sustainable development. A more sensitive approach should be adopted to policies and standards, particularly in avoiding inappropriate restrictions on the amount of development, for example by the imposition of generous off street parking standards or inappropriate amenity space standards or densities which do not have regard to the context of the development. Further guidance is given in Chapter 8 below.

4.17. Building new dwellings will not be effective in meeting the growth in housing requirements if the current stock is diminished without replacement. A Borough may include in its UDP a general presumption against the loss to other uses of existing sites and buildings in residential use, but in doing so it should take account of the need to make reasonable provision for business development within its area and the desirability of encouraging mixed uses. Boroughs and others involved in housing provision should also coordinate their activities and plans to bring empty properties into use and reduce the number of vacant dwellings. They should support the efforts being made to improve the existing stock and the environment of large estates.

4.18.   Boroughs should:

- assess the scope for conversion of existing buildings in other uses to residential use to meet changing housing needs

- set out policies and proposals to facilitate the change of use of redundant and surplus office space to housing

- review policies so that they encourage rather than hinder the conversion of existing dwellings.

Affordable housing

4.19.   A key concern of national policy is to help people find their own solutions in meeting their housing requirements, so that public sector effort can be concentrated on those in real need and who cannot get a decent home without help. In London, the private sector will continue to be the main source of new housing. Affordable housing is here taken to mean both subsidised and market housing designed for those whose incomes generally deny them the opportunity to purchase houses on the open market, as a result of the local relationship between income and market price. Boroughs should assess their need for affordable housing within this definition. Where Boroughs consider that affordable housing can realistically only be achieved through the promotion of subsidised housing, either through the public or private sector, it should be made clear how the relevant policies and proposals will address that need. At the same time, adequate allowance must be made for other market housing requirements.

4.20.   The planning system can make a contribution to meeting housing needs by ensuring a supply of new housing units and by encouraging a mix of housing types when considering applications. In London, it is recognised that authorities wish to have specific policies for affordable housing in their UDPs. This is best implemented by taking a clear and consistent view of the needs of the Borough in the context of London as a whole. Each Borough should justify such policy by reference to its assessment of local needs, in addition having regard to more general information on London's housing. Boroughs Housing Strategy Statements should be an important source of information. Authorities in the Thames Gateway area should also consider the additional information set out in the Planning Framework for that area (RPG9A).

4.21.   London's need for affordable housing requires cooperative action from those involved in providing housing. Boroughs should not, however, apply any target for affordable housing as a single blanket percentage figure on each and every new housing site or proposal, as market conditions and opportunities will vary considerably by location. A better approach is for Boroughs to identify sites or areas which are particularly suitable for affordable housing, either on the basis of local need or the type of stock to be considered (including conversions from other uses), and to set out the affordable component they would seek in negotiation with developers and agencies.

Housing Needs Assessments

The use of a specific methodology for housing needs assessments is inappropriate. Circumstances and issues will vary between Boroughs and local factors should be considered. Nevertheless, there are some indicators which have been shown, by experience in the first round of UDPs, to have been generally useful in such assessments. These include the assessment of:

- tenure changes over a time series
- average house prices and rents by number of bedrooms in the owner occupied and private rented sectors
- average incomes and savings
- lettings and changes in the available stock of social housing
- the number of waiting list applicants rehoused and the type of household
- the requirements of new and existing applicants on the waiting list
- changes in the stock of private rented flats and houses in multiple occupation
- the relationship of these factors with those for London as a whole.

Further advice on the use of such assessments is given in the DoE report *Planning for Affordable Housing* (Department of the Environment 1994b) and in *A Guide to Local Housing Needs Assessment* (Chartered Institute of Housing 1993).

4.22.   Housing needs assessments should be realistic and lead to policies for affordable housing which can be achieved and are capable of implementation. Great care should be taken to avoid duplication of indicators of need in such assessments. For example, if an authority has made assessments of special needs housing, it should not include these again in its assessment of need for affordable housing. Similarly any assessments of need leading to policies for affordable housing must show that households are both in unsuitable accommodation and cannot afford market housing as otherwise there could be a substantial overestimate of need.

4.23.   Boroughs should:

- assess housing need for the Borough, having regard to the relationship between housing in the Borough and in London as a whole

- set out strategic policies for meeting housing need in the Borough, including the contribution that can be made to affordable housing needs

- identify locations and sites suitable for affordable housing

- indicate the proportion of affordable housing that will be sought on different sites in the Borough without being prescriptive.

Special needs housing

4.24.   The provision of housing for special needs is an important part of planning for the community. Groups such as the disabled, the elderly, the chronically or terminally sick, those subject to care in the community, women seeking refuge, students and those living in hostels, all have specialised housing requirements. While the planning system should not seek to impose a uniform provision, it should facilitate different types of housing to meet these needs. The incidence of special needs may vary geographically, so Boroughs need to indicate in their UDPs what definitions or categories they are using to define special needs housing. Housing policies in UDPs should be closely related to the needs identified in the Housing Strategy Statement.

4.25.   Policies for special housing should be flexible, but should encourage a mix of housing provision. It is recognised that in London some planning authorities have historically sought to require most new housing and ground floor conversions to be built to mobility standards that allow for access by disabled people. In parts of London there can be considerable movement within the housing stock, so it is important that sufficient housing is provided or adapted to meet the needs of those with disabilities. In advance of national standards being applied through Part M of the Building Regulations, Boroughs should state clearly what they wish to achieve in negotiation with

developers, and which sites and what circumstances may be most suitable for mobility and wheelchair housing, but should not be prescriptive. Any detailed description of standards should be provided in Supplementary Planning Guidance rather than in UDPs, and policies in UDPs should not require absolute conformity with them.

4.26.   Many Boroughs will also wish to have specific policies for houses in multiple occupation and hostels. Useful advice is contained in Department of the Environment Circular 12/93, which Boroughs should consider when drafting appropriate UDP policies. These could include criteria for the areas in which they are to be encouraged. Houses in multiple occupation usually accommodate more people than self contained conversions, albeit to a lower standard, but may be appropriate to meet the needs of a mobile population, students or as transitional dwellings for those seeking more permanent accommodation. Hostels (for example for essential workers like nurses) and student accommodation should be accessible on foot or by public transport to the institutions which they serve. Sheltered housing should be within easy walking distance of local shops and other local facilities.

4.27.   Boroughs should:

- clearly define the special needs for which they will present policies in the plan

- set out policies for meeting each of the special needs

- show what standards will be applied in negotiation with developers to meet the needs of the disabled

- identify sites particularly suitable for special needs housing provision, having regard to their location to other uses and transport facilities.

4.28.   Boroughs should liaise with Housing Associations as part of the planning process, particularly when considering sites and opportunities for affordable and special needs housing. It will also be important for Boroughs to consider the opportunities provided by proposals for mixed use schemes and the possible role of Associations in such schemes. However, policies and proposals in UDPs should not require any particular form of tenure. Policies should also have regard to the likely level of resources available, including taking account of the forward plans of Associations.

Gypsy sites

4.29. London attracts a substantial demand for gypsy sites particularly in outer London and to the east of inner London. Boroughs should therefore assess the accommodation required to meet gypsies' needs and include policies governing the approval of proposals for permanent or temporary caravan sites. The policies should set out clearly the criteria to be applied when considering the suitability of sites for such use and should, wherever possible, indicate where such sites may be found. UDPs should not differentiate between categories of provider when setting criteria for the location or suitability of sites.

4.30. Gypsy sites should not be located in the Green Belt, Metropolitan Open Land or other areas of open land where development is severely restricted, and their location should be within reasonable distance of local services and facilities. Proposals for gypsy sites should have regard to highway considerations and should take account of the need for a proportion of sites to allow for mixed business and residential use or for the provision of sites for business use near to those for purely residential use. UDP policies for the provision of gypsy sites will need to be flexible and should reflect the advice given in Department of the Environment Circular 1/94.

5. Town Centres and Retailing

Town centres

5.1. Town centres within London provide a sense of place and identity and a focus for a variety of activities including shopping, local services, leisure and entertainment, other commercial activities and housing. London has a dense pattern of town centres usually well served by public transport. These existing town centres will therefore continue to be the main focus for the provision of shopping and community facilities in London. In general, Government policy for town centres is to:

- sustain and enhance the vitality and viability of town centres, and to focus retail development in locations where the proximity of competing businesses facilitates competition from which all consumers should be able to benefit

- ensure the availability of a wide range of shops, services and facilities to which people have easy access

- maintain an efficient and innovative retail sector

- maximise the opportunity for shoppers and other town centre users to use means of transport other than the car.

5.2. Guidance on the national approach to planning for town centres and retailing is given in PPG6. This is applicable to London, but needs to be applied with care as London has many centres performing different functions. PPG6 sets out a sequential approach for preferred locations. The first preference should be for sites in established town centres, but if suitable sites are not available or cannot be made available, edge of centre sites should be considered. Such sites should be used to reinforce the centre and enhance its accessibility by public transport but, in certain locations, may have a role in urban regeneration. Out of centre developments are only likely to be acceptable:

- where existing centres are incapable of providing good retailing opportunities

- where the scale, type and location of such developments would not undermine the vitality and viability of those existing centres

- in locations that can be well served by public transport (either existing or proposed).

5.3. Town centres have a range of functions as illustrated in Table 5.1. In London, each centre provides a unique blend of functions and strengths and not all centres have the same characteristics and opportunities. In PPG6, development plans have been given the role of setting out the range and hierarchy of centres in order to focus new retail and other development. The Secretary of State considers that this cannot be satisfactorily undertaken for London UDPs by Boroughs in isolation. He therefore looks to LPAC and the Boroughs jointly to provide the framework which should be reflected in the strategic policies of the UDP. LPAC has indicated a hierarchy or "network" of centres and the Secretary of State commends the description of centres set out in Tables 5.1 and 5.2 (derived from LPAC and GOL research) as a basis for considering the future of centres and drafting appropriate policies and proposals in UDPs.

5.4. The location of centres down to "Major Centres" as indicated by LPAC is illustrated in Figure 5.1. The hierarchy on which this is based must not be regarded as rigid, rather it is a description of centres at the present on the basis of defined criteria. In the future, some centres may increase their position in any hierarchy, while others may revert to a more local role. Planning activities should seek to guide the future of centres in the light of continuing realistic assessments rather than attempt to maintain a centre at any particular position in the hierarchy. Figure 5.2 shows the distribution of major retail developments (A1) granted across London in recent years.

Table 5.1 Range of Functions in a Town Centre

- **Market places:** retailing forms the heart of most centres including comparison, convenience and specialist functions
- **Business centres:** providing workspace and employment in financial and business services, administration and perhaps manufacturing and distribution, as well as sometimes the 'incubators' for new enterprise
- **Educational, health and fitness resources:** most centres have schools, colleges, training centres and there are universities in larger centres as well as doctors, dentists, clinics and hospitals, gyms, sports clubs, swimming pools and health clubs
- **Meeting places:** whether in the open air or in pubs, cafes, restaurants, clubs of all kinds or more formally in societies, conferences, community or religious groups
- **Arts, culture and entertainment zones:** with libraries, museums, galleries, theatres, cinemas, concert halls, and amusement venues, possibly supported by a series of festivals or other events
- **Places to visit:** often having historic or specialist buildings, unique views or well known sites or events
- **Transport hubs:** providing interchange and connections to local, regional, national and in some cases international services
- **Residential areas:** with town centre accommodation often most suited for students and single people or for the elderly.

Source: Department of the Environment 1994c.

Table 5.2 Types of London Town Centres

- **International Centres** are major concentrations of wide ranging specialist or comparison shopping in competition with equivalent centres in other countries and containing shops and facilities with a significant international appeal in terms of customer profile
- **Metropolitan Centres** are presently characterised as outstanding shopping centres in outer parts of London with wide catchment areas covering several Boroughs and authorities outside London. They typically have more than 100,000 m^2 of total retail floorspace and 60,000 m^2 of comparison shopping floorspace. They offer a high level and range of comparison shopping including multiple retailers and several department stores. They also have a significant range of employment and service functions and most have developed complementary activities which draw in people outside peak shopping hours
- **Regional Shopping Centres** are major concentrations in excess of 50,000 m^2 of high quality wide ranging specialist or comparison shopping, generating a substantial proportion of turnover from an area covering several Boroughs and areas outside London
- **Major Centres** are typically closer together than those in the metropolitan category, and are characteristic of Inner London. Their attractiveness for retailing has depended on maintaining a mix of both comparison and convenience shopping. They usually have at least 50,000 m^2 of retail floorspace. Some centres have developed specialist roles in addition to their general retailing functions. With sizeable local catchment areas, many of these centres have established cultural and entertainment facilities
- **District Centres** have traditionally provided convenience goods and services for local customers. They typically range in size from 10,000 to 50,000 m^2. Comparison shopping floorspace rarely exceeds 50% of the total. Their basic attraction is that they are easy and pleasant for local people to use. Some have attracted individual specialist shops or functions such as restaurants
- **Neighbourhood** or **Local Centres** have traditionally provided local services for local customers.

Source: LPAC 1995d.

Large centres

5.5. The interrelationship of centres with transport and regeneration activity will be important. Metropolitan and regional centres in particular will cater for a large number of customers and will need to be accessible to a wide catchment area. They should therefore be able to be reached from near and far by effective public transport as well as providing good access from the major road network and short term parking. In areas of regeneration, intensive redevelopment may add population and economic activity which should be served by accessible facilities. If, as a result of planning policy and regeneration, levels of population and employment in London increase, then it is likely that some centres may be able to rise up the hierarchy. However, the continuing presence of retail warehouse facilities and proposals already in the planning pipeline may restrict the opportunities for retail growth in some centres.

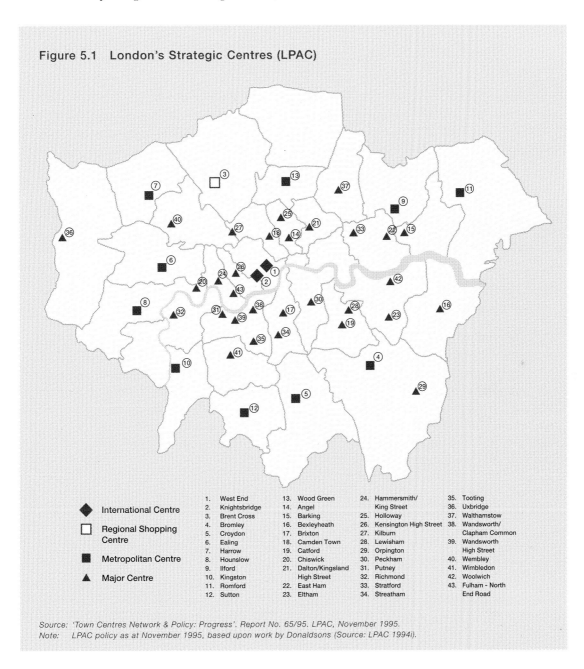

Figure 5.1   London's Strategic Centres (LPAC)

◆	International Centre
☐	Regional Shopping Centre
■	Metropolitan Centre
▲	Major Centre

1.	West End	13.	Wood Green	24.	Hammersmith/	35.	Tooting
2.	Knightsbridge	14.	Angel		King Street	36.	Uxbridge
3.	Brent Cross	15.	Barking	25.	Holloway	37.	Walthamstow
4.	Bromley	16.	Bexleyheath	26.	Kensington High Street	38.	Wandsworth/
5.	Croydon	17.	Brixton	27.	Kilburn		Clapham Common
6.	Ealing	18.	Camden Town	28.	Lewisham	39.	Wandsworth
7.	Harrow	19.	Catford	29.	Orpington		High Street
8.	Hounslow	20.	Chiswick	30.	Peckham	40.	Wembley
9.	Ilford	21.	Dalton/Kingsland	31.	Putney	41.	Wimbledon
10.	Kingston		High Street	32.	Richmond	42.	Woolwich
11.	Romford	22.	East Ham	33.	Stratford	43.	Fulham - North
12.	Sutton	23.	Eltham	34.	Streatham		End Road

Source: 'Town Centres Network & Policy: Progress'. Report No. 65/95. LPAC, November 1995.
Note: LPAC policy as at November 1995, based upon work by Donaldsons (Source: LPAC 1994i).

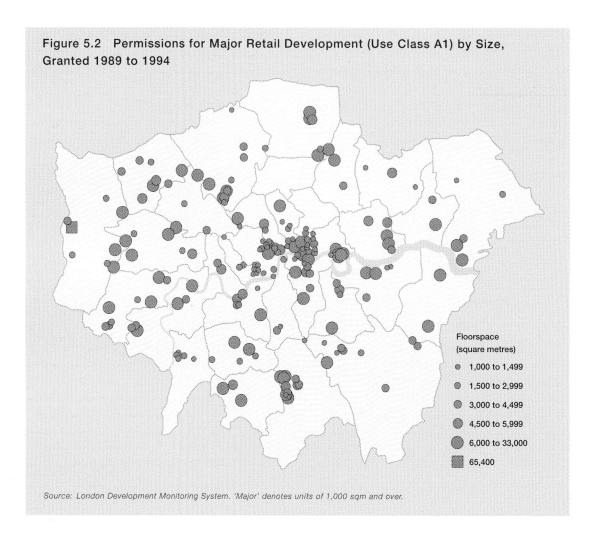

Figure 5.2 Permissions for Major Retail Development (Use Class A1) by Size, Granted 1989 to 1994

Floorspace
(square metres)

1,000 to 1,499

1,500 to 2,999

3,000 to 4,499

4,500 to 5,999

6,000 to 33,000

65,400

Source: London Development Monitoring System. 'Major' denotes units of 1,000 sqm and over.

5.6. The Secretary of State continues to recognise the concern of outer London boroughs about the impact on their town centres of proposals for new free standing shopping centres or large scale indoor leisure developments near or outside the London boundary that are almost exclusively dependent on the private car. He reaffirms that there is no place for major retail development either in the Green Belt or on Metropolitan Open Land (MOL). Authorities on the edge of London, both within and outside London, should cooperate in coordinating planning, transport and parking policies affecting the vitality and viability of town centres in their areas. They should also have regard to the effects of development proposals in their own and neighbouring centres. In the Thames Gateway area, the Planning Framework (RPG9a) provides additional guidance. Within London the regional shopping centre of Brent Cross should be supported, but any future development should be linked to an enhanced role for public transport to serve its catchment area. Near major transport interchanges serving international traffic, there may be scope for specialist outlets to serve long distance travellers and support tourism.

5.7. Because of the need to encourage continued investment in town centres and the likelihood that a dense urban area such as London will never be able to cater for unrestricted access by the car, particular care will need to be taken over the granting of permissions for large car-based retail warehouses and convenience stores. In some cases it will be appropriate to encourage mixed use schemes, especially if residential land values encourage redevelopment with a high component of housing. Authorities should seek to limit the ranges of goods sold in retail warehouses and to give preference to trips which need to be made by car or van to collect bulky and heavy goods. While car based food shopping is popular, the continued trend towards car trips may not be sustainable if it is at the expense of facilities within walking distance or close to public transport. Where public transport from a range of destinations cannot be secured at large convenience stores, encouragement should be given for the provision of smaller stores in town centres. Restricting the provision of free parking to limit demands at out of centre locations may help to shift the balance back to existing centres. It will be important to recognise that where car parking provision is allowed for, the maximum opportunity should be taken to ensure the sharing of such a facility between the various retail and other uses at such locations.

Local centres

5.8. Neighbourhood and district centres may be particularly vulnerable to the expansion of shopping facilities in larger centres or in out of centre locations. A degree of change must be accepted, and authorities should take a realistic view of the fortunes of different areas. The maintenance of local shopping facilities to serve nearby areas is important but in London, where even the Metropolitan Centres are relatively well accessible by public transport, it is unrealistic to assume that past patterns of shopping can continue indefinitely into the future. Policies will need to be flexible towards change of use, especially where shopping parades are currently run down or where there is a large proportion of vacant or underused space. It may be appropriate to encourage community, workspace and residential uses to bring back life, accepting that shopping floorspace may need to be reduced.

5.9. Boroughs should seek to maintain convenience shopping catering for local needs, including meeting the needs of the disabled and those without access to a car or who wish to use public transport. Much can be achieved through design, layout and traffic management, and with the active participation with the private sector to ensure easy access to shops by foot or from public transport, disabled parking spaces or taxis. Public transport should be able to penetrate centres, and the design of public transport stops and parking should encourage safety and security. Particular care will need to be taken on the assessment of applications for new local convenience shopping, for example at petrol stations, to ensure that the facilities are able to serve the local population without access to cars as well as the car borne shopper and that the viability and vitality of existing centres are not threatened. Some smaller centres may be suitable for concentration on specialist retailing, perhaps in conjunction with other development, for example the arts, education or tourism.

5.10. Boroughs should:

- set out strategic policies for their town centres based on the types of centre described in Table 5.2

- encourage the provision of appropriate retailing on sites in town centres or, if no sites are available, on sites at the edge of centres

- define the area where shopping use should be concentrated on proposals maps, following an assessment of the prospects for different centres

- review policies for out of centre retailing, identifying what level of activity is appropriate for car based sites and ensuring increased access by public transport or the concentration on types of goods where car use is necessary for bulky goods

- develop methodologies to assess the effect of new retail proposals on all levels of the shopping hierarchy in the catchment area of the proposal

- promote local centres which contain convenient shops catering for local needs and the less mobile.

LPAC should keep under review the relative strengths of centres and advise Boroughs and the Secretary of State on major changes in floorspace and catchments.

Retail and non retail uses

5.11. Town Centres are more than a collection of retailing units, which distinguishes them from many out of centre facilities. Their accessibility makes them particularly suitable for a range of uses serving the community. Often based on historic village centres or suburban railway stations, town centres in London act as a focus for a variety of activities including local services, leisure and entertainment, other commercial activities and housing. Town centres which are well used and active may help to reduce crime and vandalism, encourage a sense of community and support action to promote physical improvements. The promotion of appropriate development within town centres allows for efficient use of public transport infrastructure and facilities and helps to reduce the need to travel, particularly by car, and to achieve overall sustainable development objectives.

5.12. Town centres are good locations for small businesses or other enterprises. In those centres that contain vacant office and retail premises that seem unlikely to be reused for such purposes, conversion to other service and business uses should be encouraged. Frequently, it will be possible to identify sites for primary health care, serving the community, which should be accessible by public transport. Other uses which would benefit the community from being in town centres include education, arts, culture and entertainment, leisure, hotels, restaurants and cafes, financial and professional services, and tourism related facilities. If these activities are dispersed away from centres, unsustainable patterns of travel will result and the vitality and viability of centres will be threatened. An imaginative approach to mixed uses, together with the encouragement of viable enterprises and an active partnership with the private sector, will assist the centre to be economically productive through extensions of its "working day" and the attraction of customers to its facilities.

5.13.   There is considerable potential to increase the supply of housing within town centres by bringing vacant housing back into use, by the conversion of appropriate property or by allowing residential development on sites unlikely to be required for other uses. As well as initiatives such as "living above the shop", new forms of mixed uses, particularly "loft apartments" (living and working space combined) should be encouraged. Suitable sites will often be available for student flats and other hostels and for apartments. Where new residential opportunities can be achieved within town centres well served by public transport, planning authorities should not require onerous parking provision. In town centres, high densities should be permitted to allow the development of imaginative and economical schemes.

5.14.   Boroughs should:

- identify opportunities for changes of use and mixed use in town centres and consider the scope for increasing the provision of residential, business and other uses serving the community or enhancing the vitality and viability of the centre

- formulate policies to encourage uses serving the community and visitors including, where appropriate, policies for arts, culture and entertainment, leisure facilities, restaurants and hotels

- encourage the conversion of vacant premises to business and other service uses

- formulate policies to increase the supply of housing, hostels and live/work units, taking a flexible stance on the application of parking and other standards.

Assessing the health of town centres

5.15.   PPG6, the Department of the Environment Report on Vital and Viable Town Centres (Department of the Environment 1994c) and the LPAC/DoE Research Report on Town Centres and High Accessibility (LPAC 1994i) all provide useful guidance on a methodology to measure vitality and viability, to promote town centre strategies and to monitor the health of town centres. Following the research, LPAC and the Boroughs have been assessing the health of London's centres. This has established a useful methodology for specific use by London Boroughs, as set out below. In reviewing UDPs and strategies for the management of town centres, Boroughs should involve the private sector in assessing the role of the centres and the scope for change, renewal and diversification. As the need for consistent data is important, existing data sources should be maintained and enhanced to monitor the performance of centres.

5.16.   Boroughs should:

- undertake town centre health checks on a regular basis, at least every five years (but preferably every two)

- establish, from the health check and the review of UDPs, the roles of each centre at least down to District Centre level

- develop strategies for the management of centres and set out appropriate policies in UDPs.

Town Centres Health Checks - Objectives

The key objectives of health checks are to:

- record a standard set of information on a town centre, covering the main indicators of health and performance
- identify the principal role(s) of the centre, including any specialist roles which might be important over a wider area
- establish trends over time in some key indicators
- assess the centre in qualitative terms, from a user's point of view
- create a profile of the centre summarising the key characteristics, thereby allowing comparison with other relevant centres.

6. Transport and Development

A transport strategy for London

6.1.   In order to maintain its status as a world city, London requires a modern, efficient transport system which meets the needs of its residents, businesses and visitors while respecting and improving the environment. The Government's sustainable development strategy places the highest priority on the need to strike the right balance between the ability of transport to serve economic development and the ability to protect the environment and sustain future quality of life. The objective of this guidance in relation to transport and land use is to set out a strategic framework within which London's local authorities can develop plans which promote economic prosperity and personal accessibility for all, with less demand for travel overall and greater protection of the environment.

6.2.   In pursuit of these goals, the Government has the following strategic objectives for transport in London:

- to maintain and enhance the quality of London's international transport links

- to enhance the quality of commuter services by rail and underground

- to promote greater use of less polluting modes of transport, subject to the need to maintain competitiveness and safety

- to facilitate access to the central business districts and ease of movement within them

- to plug major gaps in the road and rail network.

The planning system has an important part to play by encouraging patterns of land-use which will reduce the need to travel and which take maximum advantage of existing or proposed public transport connections, consistent with the principles of sustainable development.

6.3.   These objectives are to be delivered through a balanced programme of transport investment, complemented by appropriate policies to be pursued by central Government, local authorities, public transport operators and other bodies, including the Traffic Director for London and the Parking Committee for London. Further details of this strategy are given in the Government's *Transport Strategy for London*. This chapter describes local authorities' general responsibilities for transport and land use, the specific role that local authorities should play with regard to the development of London's transport infrastructure and particular modes of transport, and guidance on parking policies and on access for people with disabilities.

The Transport Strategy for London

The strategy, set out in more detail in the *Transport Strategy for London*, embraces:

- the active promotion of walking, cycling and public transport as alternatives to car use
- measures to reduce the reliance on the private car and restrain its use; in particular, not to encourage car commuting into central London
- major investment both in the existing public transport infrastructure and, where appropriate, new lines to meet increasing demands and to serve economic regeneration
- continued investment in the region's strategic road network to provide accessibility for longer distance and commercial traffic and to allow environmental improvement on more local roads
- a comprehensive programme of traffic management measures aimed at relieving congestion, improving the environment and improving conditions for all road users as part of a balanced strategy
- limited new road construction linked to improving orbital movements and to service areas earmarked for regeneration
- the use of land use planning to reduce the overall need to travel
- the air quality strategy which is being developed under the Environment Act 1995.

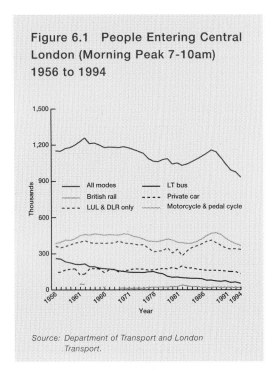

Figure 6.1 People Entering Central London (Morning Peak 7-10am) 1956 to 1994

Legend:
All modes — LT bus
British rail — Private car
LUL & DLR only — Motorcycle & pedal cycle

Source: Department of Transport and London Transport.

Local authorities, transport and land use

6.4. In partnership with other agencies and with the private sector, London local authorities can use their dual responsibilities for local transport and land use planning to make the most of opportunities offered by integrating decisions in both areas. The introduction of the "package approach" to central government support of local transport investment has increased flexibility to local authorities to achieve this. In seeking out opportunities for development Boroughs should:

- identify locations and allocate sites for development which would be consistent with generating less total travel, promoting the use of public transport and other non-car modes, creating greater opportunities for activity based on forms of transport other than the car and reducing the journey length of those trips which are made by car

- assist in the furtherance of development proposals which facilitate new public transport links, stations or interchanges, provide for non-car modes, avoid the need to provide new road capacity and bring in financial contributions from the private sector as appropriate

- allocate sites at public transport nodes for uses that can be well served by public transport

- in larger schemes plan for the provision of high quality public transport to and within the site

- where practicable, ensure freight access to new industrial development by rail or water, as well as by road

- carry out an assessment of the transport impact of development proposals, to determine how access to particular developments can be gained as far as possible by means other than the private car, requiring developers to undertake assessments in more detail when making applications, according to the size of the development (The Institution of Highways and Transportation has published guidelines (Institution of Highways and Transportation 1994) which should be used to assist assessment.)

- develop complementary land use and transport policies which maintain and enhance the viability and vitality of town centres.

Figure 6.1 shows the number of people entering Central London by various modes and figure 6.2 shows the modal split for all trips in London.

The coordinated development of London's transport networks

6.5. The Government does not directly control the development of all transport infrastructure in London. Given the overall objective of achieving modal switch away from the car onto other modes and the practical aspects of managing and developing transport networks, it is important that all those involved in planning and delivering transport programmes act in partnership and coordinate their activities. The Government, through the Minister for Transport in London, and the Government Office for London, has a role in assisting and promoting this coordination. London Boroughs and LPAC have an important coordinating role both at a strategic level in taking forward London-wide projects and at a local level, in partnership with public transport operators, developers and others, in promoting integrated local transport strategies which meet local needs. The Local Agenda 21 process is a further means for local authorities to widen cooperation on the development of such strategies by bringing in the views of communities and local interest groups.

6.6. The preparation of UDPs in London requires

a wide appreciation of developments within the transport field. The following sections consider policies and programmes applying to each mode in turn. Information about travel in London is available from the findings of LATS (the London Area Transport Surveys) (London Research Centre with Department of Transport 1994).

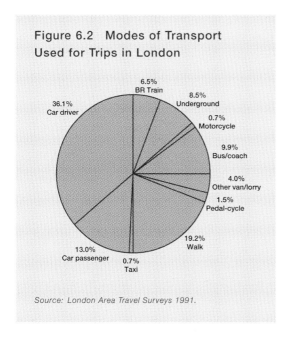

Figure 6.2   Modes of Transport Used for Trips in London

6.5%
BR Train

8.5%
Underground

36.1%
Car driver

0.7%
Motorcycle

9.9%
Bus/coach

4.0%
Other van/lorry

1.5%
Pedal-cycle

19.2%
Walk

13.0%
Car passenger

0.7%
Taxi

Source: London Area Travel Surveys 1991.

Public Transport

6.7.   London already enjoys one of the most extensive public transport systems of any capital city in the world. Map 5 shows the fixed track routes only. The constraints imposed by the road network are countered by the opportunities for travel by public transport as an alternative to private vehicles. In areas within London which are well served by public transport or where improvements can be made there should be substantial potential for slowing the rate of traffic growth by encouraging greater use of public transport and achieving a shift away from car use, especially for commuting trips. Within its own capital programmes, the Government recognises the wider economic, environmental and social benefits of investing in public transport schemes, both in new facilities to capture traffic which goes by road or which serves major development areas, and in schemes to enhance the performance of the existing network.

6.8.   The Government's objectives for public transport in London are therefore:

• to maximise the environmental and economic benefits of serving London's transport needs by

public modes in preference to the private car and improve the attractiveness of all forms of public transport to provide a viable alternative to the private car and secure modal shift

• to support new rail infrastructure where justified, both in response to demand and to assist regeneration

• to modernise the existing rail system, through investment programmes covering refurbishment and signalling systems and by maintaining and increasing the safety and efficiency of their operation

• to support a comprehensive network of bus priority measures

• to ensure that public transport operators, in conjunction with local authorities and the private sector, coordinate their activities to provide passengers with an integrated public transport network which allows easy interchange between bus, rail, underground, cycle and foot, and takes account of the needs of people with mobility difficulties

• to allow public transport operators, in the context of the framework provided by this Guidance and by the UDP, the maximum ability to provide users with a system which meets their needs.

Achieving these objectives will come about through the work of the various public transport operators and related organisations.

6.9.   Boroughs should:

• work in partnership with both public transport operators and private developers in linking development sites with improved public transport infrastructure and interchange points, and in maximising developer contributions to improvements, through s106 Obligations for example.

Rail

6.10.   Railtrack has responsibility for investment in track and related infrastructure in London on the suburban rail network. The Government has been discussing with Railtrack the development of a ten-year investment programme, which resulted in the publication of Railtrack's *Network Management*

Statement in December 1995. London Underground Ltd (LUL) is responsible for the development of investment plans for Underground rail services. LUL has developed a broad portfolio of schemes to both modernise and extend the Underground, though obviously progress will depend on the availability of resources. These schemes, together with other rail projects are illustrated in Map 5 and listed in Table 6.2. LUL is also examining the scope for intermediate modes, including light rail, in outer London (London Transport Planning 1995) and further study will be undertaken on certain routes.

6.11. The Government is keen to maximise both the financial and managerial contribution that the private sector can make to the provision of transport infrastructure in London and rail investment will therefore increasingly come from joint ventures between the public and private sectors. Working in partnership with the private sector can increase the opportunities for central and local government to integrate new and improved transport infrastructure with development. Private sector operators will take an active interest in developing their programmes to meet the commercial objectives of developers as well as the Government's wider objectives.

6.12. The Government continues to regard public subsidy and investment in public transport as vital. London Transport will continue to receive grant from central Government to finance investment in the Underground rail network. The Government is committed to continue supporting passenger rail services by public subsidy provided through the Franchising Director. Railtrack is required to make a return on its investment from charges made to train operating companies. Train companies will finance these charges through both subsidy and revenue from passengers. In addition, the Government will consider providing capital grant towards new rail infrastructure, through section 56 of the Transport Act 1968.

6.13. Boroughs should assist the development of the rail network in London by:

• bringing into a coherent local framework their own development and transport plans with the plans of public transport providers, and ensuring that their plans are consistent with the promotion of public transport

• incorporating the safeguarding requirements for rail infrastructure in their UDPs

• seeking locations for developments along the routes of major rail infrastructure, particularly around stations and stops, that enhance the viability of existing and proposed public transport

• considering the use of appropriate conditions and the negotiation of planning obligations to secure an enforcement of rail and related facilities.

Buses and coaches

6.14. Road-based public transport, buses and coaches, will play an important part in meeting demands for travel in London in future as car use becomes increasingly inappropriate for journeys in London and for trips which are less suited to rail-based public transport, such as journeys in outer London where travel patterns are more dispersed. Both buses and coaches are also important for London's tourism industry. Buses serve predominantly local needs, especially for shopping, commuting and trips to school. By providing feeder services to other modes, particularly rail, they increase the ability of the public transport network to offer convenient point to point travel. Improvements to the bus network represent the most flexible means of increasing the capacity of the public transport system quickly.

6.15. London Transport Buses are responsible for procuring and subsidising bus services in London, which are provided directly by private operators. Central Government grants will continue to be available to provide support. Local authorities have an important role to play in improving bus-based public transport through the configuration and management of the existing road infrastructure. The London Bus Priority Network, developed by the Boroughs in conjunction with London Transport, the Traffic Director and the Government Office for London, will improve the reliability and competitiveness of buses (Map 6). Reallocating road capacity away from the private car to give buses priority will often be appropriate where it is possible to do so without increasing congestion or pollution.

6.16. Coaches are more suitable for longer journeys, and provide for many commuting journeys and trips by tourists. Coach services are provided commercially by the private sector, but local authorities can act to promote this form of public transport. Good quality stops and terminal facilities which interchange with rail and local bus services will help coach companies compete with the private car, by providing for easy transfer. Set down arrangements and provision for parking to cater for the different coach markets served require strategic consideration. The large tourist market for coaches, for example, means that policies for coaches need to be considered in the context of hotel provision and major traffic attractions in cooperation with neighbouring Boroughs.

6.17. While the local environmental impact of coaches can be severe, their contribution to the capacity of the public transport system between London and the rest of the country means their strategic importance should be recognised in decisions on the siting of coach facilities. Local authorities need to integrate their approach to bus and coach travel carefully into their UDPs to maximise the benefits, in terms of providing alternatives to private car use. Development planning can also assist local authorities in finding solutions to minimise the adverse impacts of buses and coaches within their areas.

6.18. Boroughs should:

• incorporate the London Bus Priority Network into UDPs and cooperate with neighbouring authorities in implementing their traffic management policies, as they affect buses and coaches

• include in plans policies which promote good access by bus and coach to new developments, such as bus stops, lay-bys and complementary facilities for those arriving by public transport to complete their journeys on foot or cycle

• integrate provision for buses with cycle routes, where appropriate

• prepare policies and proposals, complemented with traffic management plans, which can accommodate well-integrated bus and coach stop and terminal facilities, with ready access to rail stations where possible, liaising with operators on their requirements as necessary

• consider, in conjunction with LPAC, neighbouring authorities and operators, parking and routing for coaches which allows their environmental impact, particularly in town centres, to be minimised without unduly restricting access.

Roads

6.19. Increasing demands for travel by all modes of transport have come about as a direct result of higher levels of economic and social activity. Road transport has met a greater share of demands as car ownership has increased (Fig 6.3) and as the costs to the user of road transport have become lower in real terms compared to other modes. While road traffic growth in London, especially inner London, is expected to be relatively lower than in the rest of Great Britain, the potential environmental damage that this growth would cause is a matter for concern because of heavy urbanisation, the dense concentration of the road network and existing high levels of congestion. Increasing levels of traffic and congestion will also contribute significantly to levels of pollution. Figures 6.4 and 6.5 show forecast changes in the volume of traffic and average speeds from 1991 to 2011.

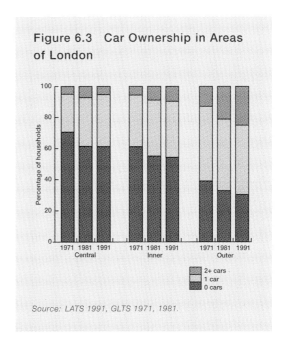

Figure 6.3   Car Ownership in Areas of London

Source: LATS 1991, GLTS 1971, 1981.

6.20. The Government recognises that it is not possible to resolve the problems of congestion and pollution through major new road construction. The Government's policy is therefore to seek to change the trends in traffic growth, through the encouragement of alternative modes. As far as possible, economic growth should be supported by public transport and other modes of transport with less environmental impact than the car.

6.21. At the same time some new development will continue to require improved access by road, particularly for goods and service deliveries. At a strategic level there is a limit to the scope for major improvements to the road network but improvements to the local road network to ease congestion and provide access to new development will remain necessary. Additionally, making the best use of London's existing road network will become increasingly important. This network provides the fundamental infrastructure for the majority of transport demands. It serves pedestrians, cyclists, taxis, commercial vehicles, service and delivery vehicles, bus operations, coach services and private cars. It provides access to national and international road, rail and air travel and to local rail systems within London. Its development, management and maintenance are closely linked with the prosperity and quality of life in London.

6.22.   The development and operation of the road network across London must be based on a coordinated and balanced appreciation of the functions of each part of the road network, and the needs of all road users, including pedestrians, cyclists, people with disabilities, bus users, car users and businesses.

6.23.   Boroughs should:

• prepare UDPs which seek to accommodate economic activity and new development in such a way as to minimise car use and ensure that a high proportion of movement needs can be met by more sustainable modes

• assess how congestion could be eased and road safety improved at accident blackspots by a mixture of restraint policies, junction improvements, traffic management measures and measures to promote public transport and improve conditions for pedestrians and cyclists

• act to constrain traffic growth in different areas by setting maximum parking standards and by targeted parking control measures

• consider the use of appropriate conditions and negotiate planning obligations to ensure the improved management of traffic and, where appropriate, traffic restraint

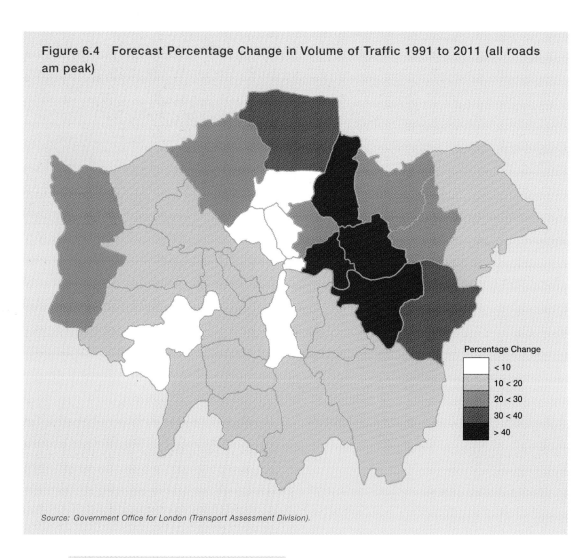

Figure 6.4   Forecast Percentage Change in Volume of Traffic 1991 to 2011 (all roads am peak)

Percentage Change

< 10
10 < 20
20 < 30
30 < 40
> 40

Source: Government Office for London (Transport Assessment Division).

- take account of the Secretary of State for Transport's aims for London's road system and his traffic management and other technical guidance (Department of Transport 1992)

- in consultation with neighbouring authorities and traffic agencies, allocate roads within their Boroughs to one of the three tiers of the London Road Hierarchy described in 6.24 - 6.31 below and in the annex to this chapter

- in the light of this allocation, compile a plan of the road hierarchy for their area within the UDP, and keep it under review.

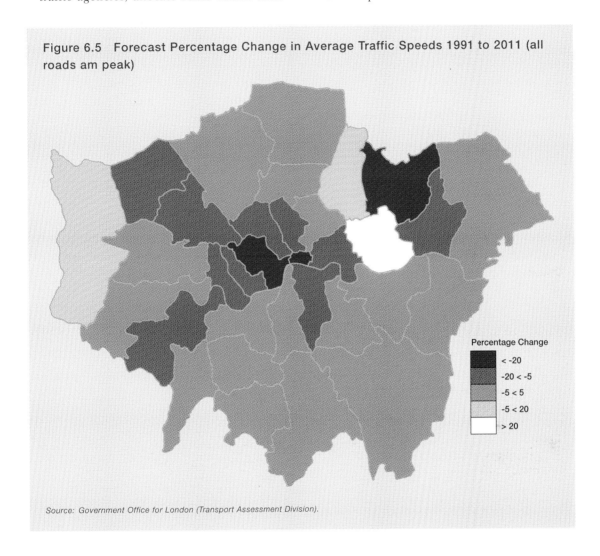

Figure 6.5   Forecast Percentage Change in Average Traffic Speeds 1991 to 2011 (all roads am peak)

Percentage Change

■	< -20
▨	-20 < -5
▤	-5 < 5
▨	-5 < 20
□	> 20

Source: Government Office for London (Transport Assessment Division).

The Road Hierarchy

6.24.   A three-tier road hierarchy has been defined for London. The structure - and its main features - are set out in the Annex at the end of this chapter. Tier 1 of the hierarchy - the strategic road network - consists of Motorways, Primary Routes and Priority (Red) Routes. The Secretary of State for Transport is the highway and traffic authority for most of these roads. As routes of national or regional importance, this tier serves to:

- ensure that London has effective road connections to national and international transport networks

- provide longer distance and commercial road traffic with suitably attractive routes throughout the region.

The motorway and primary route network is shown in Map 4.

6.25.   Given the constraints on new road construction described above, and the overall policy objective of promoting the use of public transport, priorities for development of strategic routes include:

- to focus major road improvements on strategic routes, particularly orbital routes in outer

London, in view of the wider economic and environmental benefits such improvements bring

- to relieve congestion on the strategic road network, by maximising the efficient operation of the existing system demonstrating benefits for all categories of road user, including users of road based public transport

- to tackle accident blackspots and thereby contribute to the national target for the reduction in road casualties

- to take account of Government's objectives to encourage development in the east of London especially in Docklands, the Thames Gateway and the Lee Valley.

6.26. Making the best use of the existing strategic road network will be assisted by improved traffic management and control. Under the Road Traffic Act 1991, the Government has appointed the Traffic Director for London to implement, maintain and monitor traffic management measures on the network of Priority (Red) routes (Map 6). Boroughs are already working closely with the Traffic Director in the development of Red Route Local Plans.

Aims of the Traffic Director for London

- to improve the movement of all classes of traffic on the red route network
- to provide special help for the efficient movement of buses
- to reduce the impact of congestion and improve the local environment
- to provide better conditions for pedestrians and cyclists
- to do so without encouraging further car commuting into central London.

6.27. Boroughs, in their UDP's, should enhance the effectiveness and support the development of the strategic road network by:

- planning for development at locations away from trunk roads and red routes (further guidance on the relationship between trunk roads, red routes and development is given in Appendices 2 and 3)

- including as proposals all trunk road schemes proposed by the Highways Agency in its national and regional programmes within and adjacent to the plan area as notified by the Agency

- developing parking policies which support the Traffic Director for London's objective of not increasing car commuting into central London

- including details of red routes within UDPs

- planning measures which remove short distance traffic from strategic routes and encourage longer distance and commercial traffic to make use of strategic routes

- recognising the status of non-trunk primary routes and red routes within and adjacent to the plan area.

6.28. Tier 2 of the hierarchy - the network of London Distributor Roads - provides a district distributor function. These roads serve to provide movements within London that cross Borough boundaries and so consistency of definition is needed. The objectives for such roads are largely for individual Boroughs to determine, providing the district distributor function is maintained and subject to:

- the overall policy framework described in this chapter

- the requirement to notify the Traffic Director for London of any changes to the network of roads designated under the Local Government Act 1985, or of any changes to roads affecting that network

- the need to ensure consistency of treatment of all roads which cross Borough boundaries, through consultation with neighbouring Boroughs.

6.29. Enforcement of sensible traffic and parking regulations on roads in this tier will be crucial to their various functions. Boroughs will need to agree the definition of Tier 2 roads with the Government Office for London, the Highways Agency, the Traffic Director for London and adjacent Boroughs. The proposals for the London Bus Priority Network largely apply to roads in this tier, and such proposals should be included in UDPs. Boroughs are responsible for determining which other roads in their ownership should be allocated to this tier.

6.30.   Tier 3 of the hierarchy covers local distributor roads and access roads, about 85% of the total road network. Policies and objectives for this category are entirely for the local authorities to determine within the Government's overall objective that these roads, many of which serve residential areas or town centres and other environmentally sensitive areas where pedestrian movements are a priority, are kept free as far as is sensible of traffic which should be taken by primary and district distributor roads. Access roads in particular will be suitable for traffic calming and traffic restrictions.

6.31.   Within this tier Boroughs should:

• ensure that full consultation is held with local interests on policies applying to these roads

• in considering traffic restraint or calming, ensure that the viability of road based public transport is not jeopardised and ensure that access for emergency services is maintained.

Walking

6.32.   Boroughs have the major responsibility for providing high quality facilities for pedestrians. A better quality environment for pedestrians can encourage more people to make trips on foot. This is essential to the daily life of every resident and visitor to London, and can make a significant contribution towards a more sustainable transport system. Walking constitutes an important mode in its own right, as well as being the mode at the end of many other journeys, particularly those made by public transport.

6.33.   In those areas where pedestrian movements are most prevalent, such as town centres, Boroughs need to ensure that the right balance is struck between pedestrians' needs and the needs of other road users. In some areas schemes to restrict or remove traffic, such as traffic calming or pedestrianisation, will be appropriate as a means of creating better conditions. They need to be coupled with complementary traffic management measures, and access for both public transport and businesses, as appropriate.

6.34.   The close proximity of many varied land uses in London means that a greater proportion of trips can be undertaken on foot than in less densely built up areas. Many walking trips will cross Borough boundaries and local authorities should make

provision for pedestrian routes, including appropriate signing, in cooperation with other authorities. Established routes form a basis upon which new ones might be developed, to facilitate movement for different journey purposes. Further guidance is given in Chapter 7 (see Fig 7.2). Examples of the scope for developing routes are the provision of safe routes to schools, and the gaining of public access to links between green spaces, canals and riversides. Links with the public transport network should be maximised to promote integrated journeys.

6.35.   In including policies and proposals which promote safe walking within their UDPs, Boroughs should ensure that:

• new developments and transport interchanges allow ready access for pedestrians as well as other road users

• new land use patterns allow for a greater number of journeys between activities to be made by foot

• areas and routes set aside for pedestrians are as far as is practicable fully accessible and do not create obstacles for people with disabilities

• proposed walks are integrated as far as possible with other networks, including cycle and bus networks, and allow access to public transport stops and stations

• they have considered the scope for traffic free routes in London, coordinating access to waterside routes including the Thames path and longer distance routes.

Cycling

6.36.   Cycling is economical and efficient, environmentally friendly and healthy. Almost two thirds of all trips in London are under 5 km in length and many of these could reasonably be made by cycle if convenient and safe conditions were to be created. There is therefore a significant potential for modal shift away from car use to cycle use.

6.37.   The Government has adopted a new approach to cycling in line with its sustainable development strategy. This is supported by the commitment to implement the London Cycle Network, to be taken forward by the Boroughs, with support from the Government Office for London, the Highways Agency and the Traffic Director for London. The main aim of this network is to make travel by bicycle in London easier and safer. It will incorporate a safe, convenient and conspicuous network of routes linking local centres and providing for longer distance journeys across the whole of London. The network will help cyclists avoid main roads and provide extra protection where heavily trafficked streets and busy junctions are unavoidable.

6.38. As with walking, Boroughs need to ensure that the promotion of cycling is fully reflected in UDP policies and proposals, by:

- including policies and proposals which will lead to improved conditions for safe walking and cycling

- incorporating the proposed London Cycle Network in UDPs and ensuring new developments foster and do not jeopardise its implementation

- ensuring that new developments allow ready access for cyclists and incorporate reasonable levels of secure cycle parking facilities in appropriate locations, particularly at bus and rail interchanges

- encouraging new patterns of development which allow for journeys to be made more easily by cycle

- including improvements for cycling in Proposal Maps.

Taxis

6.39. London's taxis (licensed hackney carriages) perform an important function, particularly in central and inner London and generally for short trips. They have the advantage over the private car that an individual can travel by road without the need for a car parking space and can gain speedy access to other public transport. This can increase the accessibility of other forms of public transport thereby reducing the need for people to travel by private car. Taxis allow short trips within London to be undertaken efficiently by the business community, when time is at a premium. They also provide an important and distinctive service to London's tourists and visitors, with 40% of all taxi trips made by non-residents. Increasingly they provide a service for people with disabilities. Minicabs can also perform a valuable function in relation to a range of trips, including shopping trips, evening social trips, and access to public transport.

6.40. Like other motor vehicles, taxis and minicabs can cause environmental harm, so proposals to manage their movements which are sensitive to these disbenefits are necessary. Boroughs should:

- ensure that adequate facilities are provided for taxis in major developments, at public transport interchanges and in town centres, integrated with proper access for pedestrians and people with disabilities

- consider the use by taxis of bus priority facilities on a scheme by scheme basis.

Airports and heliports

6.41. The airports within Greater London, Heathrow and London City, with smaller sites at Biggin Hill and RAF Northolt serving business aviation, play a major role in the UK's transport infrastructure and have a significance beyond the geographical area covered by this Guidance. These airports make an important contribution to the competitiveness of the UK economy and its attractiveness to both domestic and foreign investment. Airports also have a positive impact on the local economy. Conversely, many people within London will use airports such as Gatwick, Stansted and Luton beyond its boundary. National airports policy therefore plays an important role in the planning process.

6.42. The last major statement of the Government's national airports policy was in 1985 (HM Government 1985). The approach set out then - in which it is for the owners and operators of airport facilities to plan for their development, and to bring forward applications to be considered within the planning system - remains largely relevant today. In view of the benefits to the UK economy the Government does not wish unnecessarily to constrain airport growth in London, where it makes economic, environmental and social sense. Nor does it wish to intervene without clear justification in the private sector's judgement on where air services are provided.

6.43. Air traffic has a potential global environmental impact and the Government recognises that airport facilities can have significant environmental impact. It is therefore essential that best use is made of existing facilities and it is generally preferable for development to take place at existing sites. In recognition of the continuing strong demand for air travel in the South East, an independent working group (RUCATSE) was set up by the Government in 1990 to undertake work on a number of possible sites for additional runway capacity in the South East which had been identified as feasible in air traffic control terms (Department of Transport 1993). The purpose was to produce, without prejudice, a technical assessment of options from which comparisons could be made. Following the group's report the Government announced its response in February 1995. In this, the Secretary of State for Transport said that in view of their severe environmental impacts, no further work should be undertaken on the RUCATSE options for new runways at Heathrow and Gatwick. He also announced additional studies to take forward the findings of RUCATSE. These will examine the possible capacity gains that had been identified by the Heathrow Runway Capacity Enhancement Study, the possibility of less environmentally damaging options for development, such as a close parallel runway at Gatwick, and surface access to and between London's airports (The London Airports Surface Access Study is described in Chapter 2.).

6.44. As with airport development, it is for private sector operators to make proposals for new heliport development, whether through enhancement of existing facilities or the creation of new sites. The Government published the *London Heliport Study* in March 1995 (Department of Transport 1995). The report does not make recommendations about the siting of new development but in considering the operational suitability of a range of six sites the study did identify a number of technical issues which would need to be addressed at any future planning inquiry. Heliport development brings both economic benefits and environmental impacts, particularly noise. In reviewing UDPs, Boroughs should bear in mind similar considerations for the development of heliport facilities to those applying to airport facilities and reach a balanced view on the economic and environmental impacts.

6.45. Boroughs should:

- address the consequences of the use made of currently authorised aviation facilities

- consult airport operators about their forecasts for such facilities, to inform their plans and consider levels of air traffic that might reasonably be expected in the foreseeable future (in particular with reference to PPG24 in relation to noise sensitive development)

- develop with airport operators, public transport operators, car parking operators and others a common approach to, and strategies to deal with, the surface access implications of existing and planned growth at airports, in order to promote public transport and reduce car use.

Parking policy

6.46. A comprehensive approach to car restraint through London Borough's parking policies forms part of the overall strategy to discourage traffic growth and promote modal shift. Parking policy should complement traffic calming and other restraint measures introduced away from the strategic network. Boroughs should seek a balanced approach which recognises the legitimate need for parking to meet economic objectives and enhance the respective position of their areas but set that against the environmentally damaging effects of traffic movement and the impact of parked cars. It will be necessary to consider the interaction between all forms of parking in establishing this balance and to work towards the progressive restraint of car use where alternatives are or can be made available.

6.47. In arriving at parking standards Boroughs will need to make a judgement which takes account of:

- the current and planned availability of public transport services providing an alternative to the car for access to the area

- existing and forecast traffic levels in the area and the level of traffic restraint considered appropriate

- existing and planned restrictions of on street parking through controlled parking zones.

6.48. Figures 6.6 and 6.7 illustrate measures of public and private transport accessibility across London. Local assessments should be undertaken to take account of differences in accessibility within Borough boundaries. The adoption of a methodology to define public transport levels of accessibility will be valuable in demonstrating the parts of Boroughs where more sustainable development can take place and in indicating the scope for improvements to different modes of transport. The Public Transport Accessibility Index developed by the London Borough of Hammersmith and Fulham is one means by which local authorities can develop objective assessments of those areas well served by public transport in their areas. The

Secretary of State requests LPAC to keep these assessments under review and report on good practice.

6.49.   Boroughs should:

• set out strategic policies for restricting parking in line with the objectives of this Guidance

• develop strategies for parking which incorporate the Borough's approach to off street, on street and private non-residential parking, in cooperation with neighbouring authorities

• restrict parking at new developments away from existing centres and public transport which, if provided, would increase the number and length of trips by private car

• ensure that arrangements for managing and controlling parking on and off street help to preserve and enhance existing economic centres and their competitiveness in relation to out of town developments

• give priority to short term parking for shoppers rather than long term parking for commuters in town centres

• set out policies for maximum off street parking standards in relation to land uses defined by the Use Classes Order, expressed as standards for floorspace, within the guidance given in 6.51 - 6.53.

• in considering proposals for development, only permit the maximum levels set out in UDPs to be exceeded where they can be specifically justified in relation to the particular traffic generation characteristics of the development and its economic and regeneration importance, having regard to the provision of public transport and the impact on the environment of extra traffic

• establish, in cooperation with other Boroughs and with LPAC, the levels of parking required for essential operational purposes and to meet the needs of the disabled.

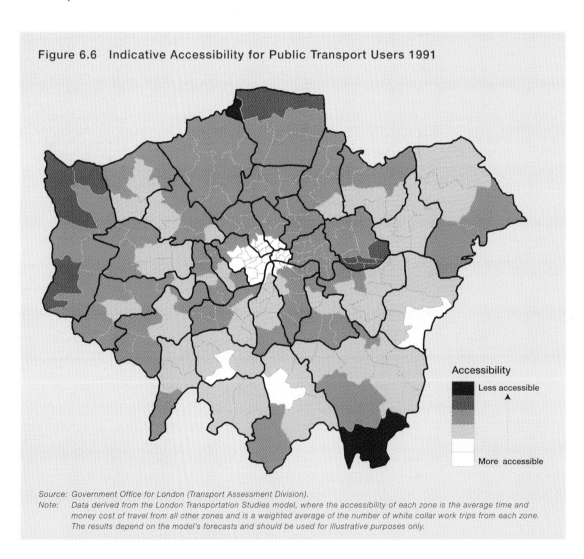

Figure 6.6   Indicative Accessibility for Public Transport Users 1991

Accessibility

Less accessible

More accessible

Source: Government Office for London (Transport Assessment Division).
Note: Data derived from the London Transportation Studies model, where the accessibility of each zone is the average time and money cost of travel from all other zones and is a weighted average of the number of white collar work trips from each zone. The results depend on the model's forecasts and should be used for illustrative purposes only.

On street parking

6.50. With the assistance of the Parking Director for London, Boroughs should work towards a comprehensive and consistent approach to on street parking restrictions, including the coordination of controlled parking zones and special parking areas. Borough parking policies if targeted on routes used by bus services can complement other measures aimed at improving bus travel. Boroughs should also seek to avoid difficulties caused by lack of coordination of controls at Borough boundaries. Further guidance on parking policies is given in the Department of Transport circular 5/92, *Traffic Management and Parking Guidance* (the revision of which the Government Office for London is currently discussing with other London organisations). The Government's national air quality strategy will also be relevant (see paragraph 9.20).

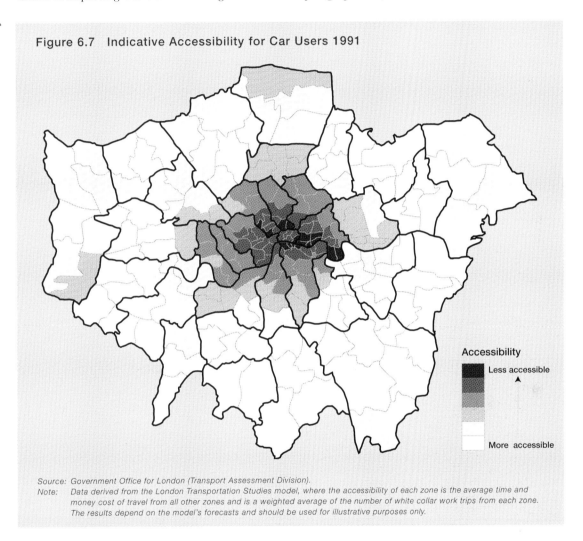

Figure 6.7 Indicative Accessibility for Car Users 1991

Accessibility

Less accessible

More accessible

Source: Government Office for London (Transport Assessment Division).
Note: Data derived from the London Transportation Studies model, where the accessibility of each zone is the average time and money cost of travel from all other zones and is a weighted average of the number of white collar work trips from each zone. The results depend on the model's forecasts and should be used for illustrative purposes only.

Off street parking

6.51. The amount of traffic generated by new developments should be minimised by placing maximum limits on the levels of off street car parking spaces permitted. Where possible, the parking provision in existing developments should be brought into line when redevelopment takes place or through negotiation. In setting maximum levels in UDPs, taking account of parking provision for operational needs, Boroughs should generally not exceed the levels set out in Table 6.1 for employment uses. It may, however, be appropriate for areas to be identified in plans where less or, exceptionally, more parking should be allowed. In these cases policies should be fully justified in relation to the land uses, highway network and public transport accessibility of the areas concerned. Although past practice has been to require parking by setting down minimum standards, reviews of UDPs should make it clear that off street non residential parking is set at a maximum in order to reduce dependence on the car.

6.52. Table 6.1 shows a range of parking standards that Boroughs should apply as maxima in future UDPs. Boroughs should convert these into specific standards for different land uses with reference to the Use Classes Order, having regard to the characteristics of different parts of their area. The figures in the table relate to employment generating uses and do not include spaces for (for example) short term use by shoppers. Boroughs should also consider other uses and discourage parking, for example by students. Parking standards should be related to a more general approach to development reflecting public transport accessibility. Where public transport accessibility is good higher densities of employment generating activities should be allowed but without increasing the number of car parking spaces.

6.53. Over time, as accessibility by public transport (or walking and cycling) is improved, it may be possible progressively to reduce parking provision. The Secretary of State requests LPAC to keep parking standards and the reassessment of public transport accessibility under review. The need for supplementary Guidance on the preparation and application of off street non residential parking standards will be considered following further consultation with LPAC and the main agencies and operators involved in the provision and management of London's public transport and traffic.

Table 6.1 Parking Standards for Employment Generating Development

Area	One off street space per m² gross floor space
Outer London	300-600
Inner London	600-1,000
Central London	1,000-1,500

Boroughs may use the OPCS definitions of Central, Inner and Outer London as an initial basis for the setting of standards. Where Boroughs set standards based on different definitions within individual UDPs, such variations should be explained.

Park & ride

6.54. Good access by public transport to many areas in London means that park and ride schemes, where car drivers are encouraged to use their cars for part of their journey, leave them at designated parking sites, and continue the rest of their journeys by rail or bus, may lead to an increase in the length and number of car trips, rather than a reduction. Nevertheless there may be scope for schemes, particularly in outer London, which provide good quality car parking away from town centres and allow car drivers to gain access by means of dedicated bus services. Boroughs should examine the scope for schemes, and where appropriate, allocate land in plans. In designing schemes they should take care not to increase the attractiveness of car use overall but rather consider park and ride only as part of a wider transport strategy aimed at reducing overall car use.

Access for people with disabilities

6.55 The Government aims to see access for disabled people continually improved. Local authorities' transport and development policies need to be consistent with this overall aim. Public transport operators in London are already subject to a range of statutory obligations to provide for the travel needs of people with disabilities. Measures already taken and current initiatives on buses, trains and taxis will significantly improve mobility and access and promote independent living. At the same time many people with disabilities will continue to depend on the private car to travel. Policies which seek to reduce car travel, in line with the Government's objectives for sustainable development, should not disadvantage the disabled. In particular local authorities should:

- in seeking mixed patterns of development which require less travel, maximise the opportunities for disabled travellers to gain access to new and existing facilities

- encourage development which provides good links to road and public transport networks especially for the disabled

- facilitate or require the provision of convenient parking facilities and easy access to buildings for disabled people, where necessary increasing parking to meet their needs, but ensuring it is not subsequently used as general parking.

Table 6.2   Investment Programmes

- **Major Public Transport schemes**

  Jubilee Line Extension
  Heathrow Express
  DLR Extension to Lewisham
  East London Line Extensions
  Croydon Tramlink
  Thameslink 2000
  Channel Tunnel Rail Link
  CrossRail
  Chelsea Hackney Line

- **Local Authority promoted Rail schemes**

  Additional stations on the West London Line
  Stratford Station Eastern Concourse
  Barking Gospel Oak line improvements
  Heathrow North and South Stations - SWELTRAC/BAA/Railtrack

- **Major Trunk Road Improvements**

  A12 Hackney - M11 Link Road
  A13 Improvements
  A406 North Circular Road improvements
  A40 Upgrading

- **Major Local Authority TSG schemes under construction**

  A2016 Erith/Thamesmead Spine Road - LB Bexley
  A206 Woolwich Road Improvement - LB Greenwich
  A409 Sheepcote Road - LB Harrow
  A240 North/South Strategy - LB Kingston
  A11 Stratford Gyratory modifications - LB Newham
  A110 Nags Head Road/A1010 High Street Ponders End - LB Enfield
  A404 Harrow Road/B450 Ladbroke Grove Widening - Westminster CC and RB Kensington & Chelsea

- **London wide initiatives**

  Trunk Road Network Enhancement Projects
  Priority (Red) Route network
  Local Authority local safety schemes
  Primary Route Network Resigning
  London Bus Priority Network
  London Cycle Network

- **Town Centre improvement and transport interchange schemes**

  Hounslow Town Centre - LB Hounslow
  A4020 Uxbridge Town Centre - LB Hillingdon
  Wood Green - LB Haringey
  Canning Town Interchange - LUL/DLR/Railtrack

- **East London River Crossings**

  Blackwall III
  Woolwich Rail Tunnel
  Combined rail and local road crossing at Gallions Reach

Further details of the programme are published in the Government's *Transport Strategy for London*

ANNEX

THE LONDON ROAD HIERARCHY

General

1. The categorisation of individual roads will be based on the functions they provide to road users and adjacent land uses. The components of the London Road Hierarchy are set out below. Table 6.3 summarises how each component influences or relates to a range of development and operational issues. Further guidance on the hierarchy is in preparation.

2. Local authorities should apply the principles set out here to their individual UDPs. Each authority is expected to compile a plan of the road hierarchy for their area, in consultation with neighbouring authorities and to keep it under review. The plan should be incorporated into the next review of the UDP.

Tier 1 - Strategic Routes of national or regional importance

3. These provide the distributor network for longer distance vehicle movements, within the area bounded by M25/A282 and the connections from all parts of Greater London to the national road network. They comprise Motorways, Primary Routes and Priority (Red) Routes. Motorways have distinctive blue regulatory and direction signs. Primary Routes have green direction signs and a London-wide programme of re-signing an updated network of primary routes is expected to be completed by 2000. Red Routes, with their distinctive regulatory signs and intensive enforcement are largely coincident with Primary Routes; they too are expected to be operational in 2000 under the powers of the Traffic Director for London from the Road Traffic Act 1991. Within Greater London strategic routes constitute about 5% of the total network by length and currently carry about 30% of traffic in terms of vehicle kilometres. Further details on individual routes in Tier 1 are available from the Government Office for London.

4. Indicative average daily traffic flows for a route to be considered for inclusion in this tier are for two of the following three Annual Average Weekday Traffic (AAWT) flows to be exceeded:

300 buses/coaches
3000 light goods vehicles
1000 medium/heavy goods vehicles

5. Routes of national or regional importance should be more attractive than other categories of roads to drivers making longer distance journeys. Within the M25 the direction signing on all primary routes is being overhauled. Most primary routes will also become Priority (Red) Routes where kerbside waiting and loading will be subject to special controls introduced by the Traffic Director for London.

6. Catering for through traffic will normally have priority over access to adjacent land uses. In accordance with PPG13, direct access on to motorways should not be permitted and direct access on to primary routes should be avoided as far as possible. However, there are locations where in addition to its primary function a route of national or regional importance has also to bear secondary functions and carry out at least some of the requirements of a lower tier road. In these circumstances, development alongside a route of national or regional importance can be considered. Guidance on potential developments alongside Trunk Roads and Priority (Red) Routes is given in Appendices 2 and 3. Nevertheless, direct access should normally be taken from a lower tier road where this option is available.

7. UDPs should include firm proposals for new or improved sections of road in this tier and an appreciation of the relevant traffic management, parking control and road maintenance regimes which are expected to apply.

Tier 2 - London Distributor Roads

8. London Distributor Roads will consist generally of existing A roads other than those in Tier 1. These roads should attract and serve drivers making journeys between and across Boroughs and to counties bordering Greater London. Adequate direction signing will be required. They constitute about 10% of the public road length within Greater London and handle about 35% of vehicular movement. Indicative average daily traffic flows for roads in this tier are for two of the following three Average Annual Weekday Traffic (AAWT) flows to be exceeded:

100 buses/coaches
1000 light goods vehicles
300 medium/heavy goods vehicles

though adjacent Boroughs may wish to agree to different indicative traffic flows for categorising Tier 2 roads.

9.   London Distributor Roads generally have to provide access to adjacent land uses, but their primary function must be to act as part of the network for through traffic around London. Boroughs will need to consider how their UDPs treat this tier within the London road hierarchy. The London Bus Priority Network is largely located on London Distributor roads; this will generally fulfil the requirement for London Distributor Roads to give priority, where appropriate, to local bus services. UDPs will also need to be consistent with the traffic management, parking control and road maintenance regimes which are expected to apply to London Distributor Roads. Guidance on potential developments alongside designated roads is given in Appendix 3.

Tier 3 - Local distributor and access roads

10.   While the majority of roads in this tier are expected to serve primarily as access roads there is the important category of Borough Distributor Road, catering primarily for movement within the Borough and based on the network of classified B and C roads. Some categories of frontage development are not suited to this category of road, particularly at critical junctions. There will be extensive latitude for Boroughs to redefine the pattern of local distributors.

11.   Indicative average daily traffic flows for a section of road to be considered as a Borough Distributor Road are for two of the following three Average Annual Weekday Traffic (AAWT) flows to be exceeded:

30 buses/coaches
300 light goods vehicles
100 medium/heavy goods vehicles

though individual Boroughs may wish to use different indicative traffic flows for defining their distributor roads.

12.   Boroughs will therefore have considerable autonomy for defining Borough Distributor and local access roads, though classified roads will still have to be notified to the Department of Transport. However in inner London there will continue to be a need for coordination between adjacent boroughs on defining Borough Distributor Roads.

13.   Many local roads will be primarily for use by residents and pedestrians. The traffic functions of local roads will often be subordinated to environmental concerns. Traffic calming measures to displace through traffic can be appropriate to local access roads. Physical measures which control excessive vehicle speeds may be appropriate to Borough Distributor Roads. Local roads will frequently provide opportunities to provide safer routes for pedal cyclists and to improve amenities for pedestrians.

Table 6.3   The Three Tier London Road Hierarchy

Tier	Description current status	Route length (kms) approx	Typical speed limit mph	Typical ADDT thousand vehicles	Primary road traffic function	Access control	Possible features for specific categories of road user	Other land use or network management considerations
Strategic routes	Motorways and high speed dual carriageway primary routes with limited frontage access and Priority (Red) Route restrictions	300	70	60-150	To attract and serve longer distance movements throughout London, particularly by commercial and public transport vehicles	General presumption against new accesses or increased use of existing accesses - see PPG13	No pedestrian or cyclist use of motorways, separate facilities where necessary; separate or segregated facilities preferred for all high speed roads	Traffic sensitive; extensive restrictions will apply to roadworks, possibly involving temporary diversion routes to lower tier roads
	Other primary routes, generally 2/3/4 lane single carriageway with Priority (Red) Route restrictions; includes Designated Routes which are also Priority (Red) Routes	300	40/60 outer London; 30/40 inner London	25-70	To provide the London component of the trunk road and primary route networks; To link London to the national road network	Lower tier road access always preferred, but where route has significant lower tier functions and no lower tier access practical, then new or improved accesses can be considered - see Appendices 2 and 3	Where route has significant lower tier functions, kerbside waiting and loading will be needed, but priority always to through traffic	
London distributor roads	A Roads outside top tier which are Designated Roads	300	30/40 outer London; 30/40 inner London	20-40	To attract and serve traffic crossing boroughs; To link centres within London to each other and to the network of national/regional routes and to attract commercial traffic away from Borough distributor and access roads; To provide attractive routes for bus services	Important that new frontage development does not significantly affect the traffic distribution function of the road	Measures to assist buses and cyclists will frequently be appropriate - the London Bus Priority Network mostly on these roads. Kerbside loading and parking required to facilitate frontage development but should not generally interfere with the traffic capacity of road junctions	Traffic sensitive; usually with peak period restrictions on roadworks
	Other A Roads/Principal Roads not in the top tier	900	30/40 outer London; 30 inner London	10-30				
Local distributor and access Roads	Borough Local Distributor Roads typically Classified B or C roads	1,600	30	5-25	To distribute traffic within a London Borough Where appropriate, to connect with the distributor roads of adjacent Boroughs	Access control will depend on local conditions, but new or intensified development will have to be commensurate with the general capacity of the distributor network	Bus priorities may be appropriate; sections may form part of the Cycle Network. Kerbside parking and loading spaces will often be appropriate	Only occasional sections will be traffic sensitive
	Local access roads typically unclassified roads	10,200	20/30	under 5	To serve frontage properties; to contribute to local amenity	Minimal restrictions commensurate with scale of development; access to larger developments may be more appropriate to Borough distributor roads	Parking controls and traffic calming appropriate to restrain extraneous traffic; special facilities may be appropriate for local bus, pedestrian or cyclist movements	

Map 4   The Strategic Road Network: Motorways and Primary Routes
after completion of London Primary Route Re-signing and new A12 and A13 routes

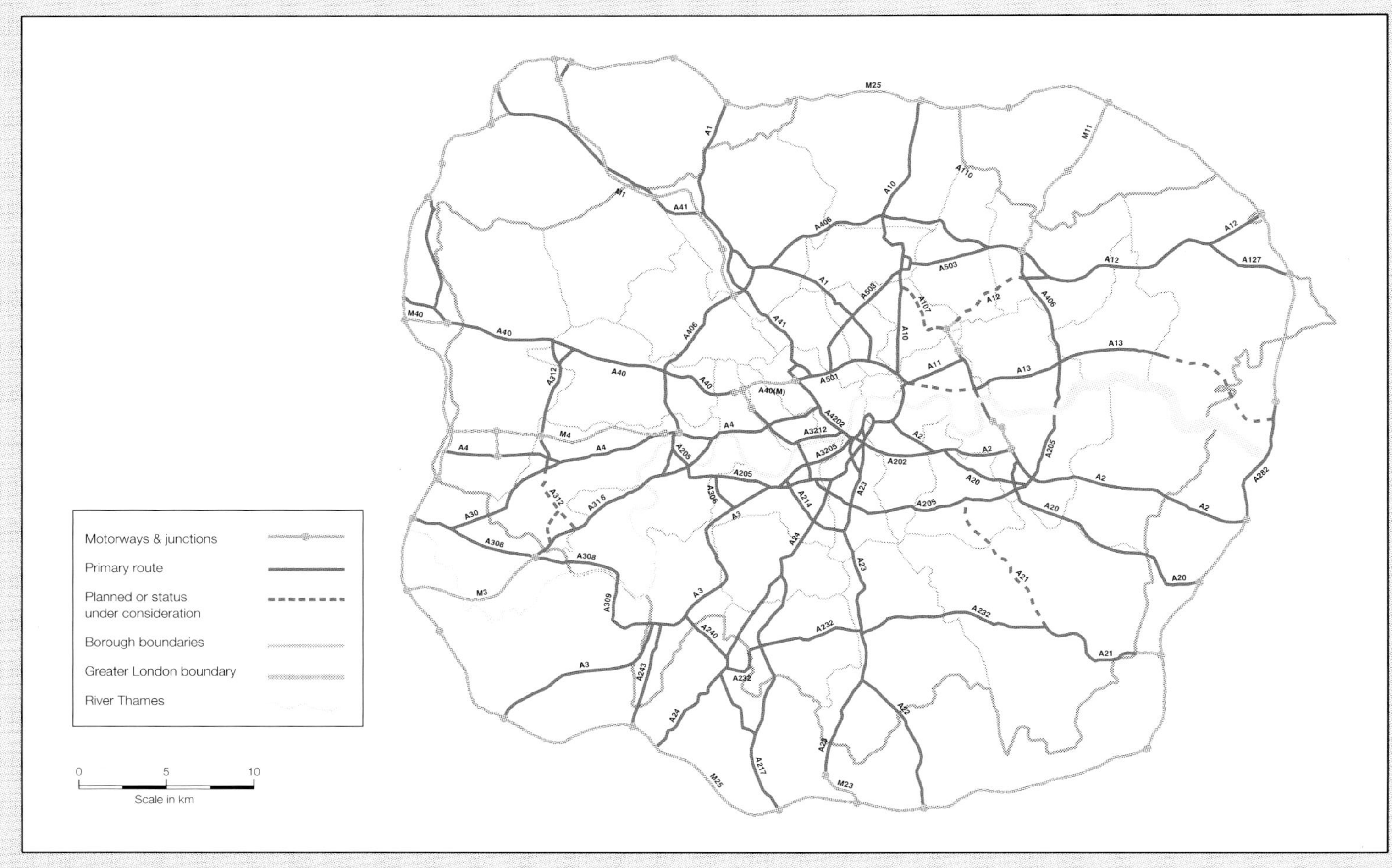

Motorways & junctions

Primary route

Planned or status
under consideration

Borough boundaries

Greater London boundary

River Thames

0   5   10
Scale in km

Map 5 Existing and Proposed Rail Lines

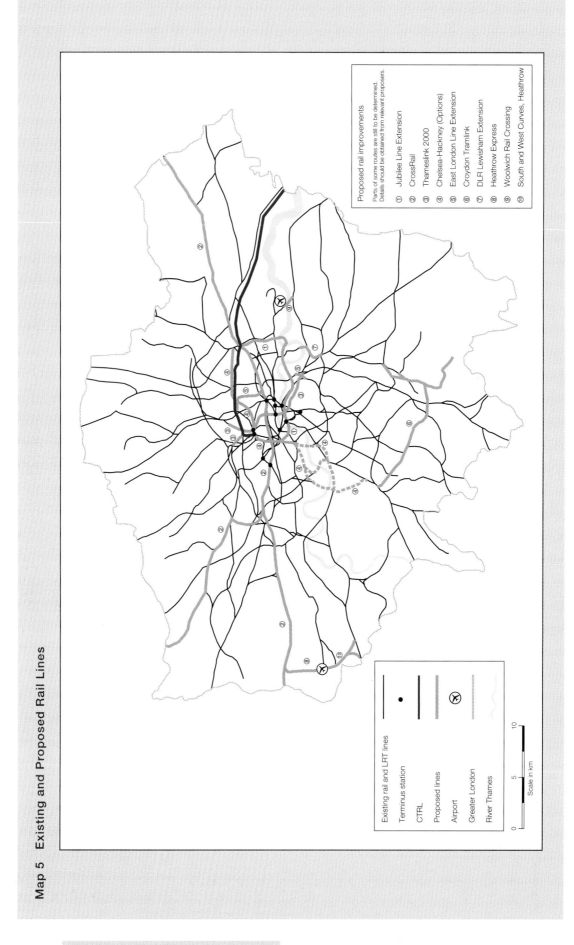

Proposed rail improvements

Parts of some routes are still to be determined.
Details should be obtained from relevant proposers.

① Jubilee Line Extension
② CrossRail
③ Thameslink 2000
④ Chelsea-Hackney (Options)
⑤ East London Line Extension
⑥ Croydon Tramlink
⑦ DLR Lewisham Extension
⑧ Heathrow Express
⑨ Woolwich Rail Crossing
⑩ South and West Curves, Heathrow

Existing rail and LRT lines
Terminus station
CTRL
Proposed lines
Airport
Greater London
River Thames

Scale in km

0   5   10

Map 6   Priority Route Networks in London

Priority 'Red' routes

Bus priority routes

Motorways & junctions

Trunk roads

Other routes

Borough boundaries

Greater London boundary

River Thames

Sources: Red routes - Traffic Director for London
            Bus priority routes - London Regional Transport
Note: Network simplified in Central Area

0   5   10

Scale in km

7. The Open Environment

7.1. One of London's greatest assets is its framework of green space and open land. It enjoys a legacy of Royal Parks, municipal parks and open spaces, private spaces and playing fields. Together with green chains, waterways, reservoirs and flooded gravel pits they provide visual contrast with the urban fabric, often with recreational and nature conservation importance. London's open spaces make a valuable contribution to the quality of the environment and the quality of life. The Green Belt has prevented the encroachment of London on its surrounding countryside, whilst the concept of Metropolitan Open Land (MOL), which was first recognised in the 1989 Guidance, has provided similar protection to large areas of open land in London. Boroughs have defined the boundaries of these areas in their UDPs (Map 7), but it is now important to maintain and enhance the quality of all of London's open areas.

7.2. If the character and value of open spaces are to be enhanced, Boroughs will need to maintain a positive approach to them. The review of UDPs provides the opportunity to analyse critically the characteristics and uses of open spaces with particular reference to their amenity value, ecological contribution and public access to them. Increasing pressures for active leisure and recreational pursuits need to be considered against the value of the areas for passive enjoyment and nature conservation. In some areas this will call for management action and partnerships. Where development is involved which requires a change in the status of the land, the necessary changes should be brought forward as an alteration to the UDP.

Green Belt

7.3. National policies and further advice on the Green Belt are set out in PPG2. For Green Belt in London the four main purposes are:

- to check the unrestricted sprawl of large built up areas

- to prevent neighbouring towns from merging into one another

- to assist in safeguarding the countryside from encroachment

- to assist in urban regeneration by encouraging the recycling of derelict and other urban land.

The Green Belt also provides opportunities for Londoners to enjoy the open countryside.

7.4. London's Green Belt is under considerable pressure in many locations by virtue of its close proximity to the built up area. Its quality is in danger of being eroded by the intensity of uses to which it may be put and the different demands made upon it. This is especially the case on the urban fringe. Recent research into landscape change in London's Green Belt has concluded that its landscape character has changed significantly and that in places its landscape quality has deteriorated (LPAC 1993). This suggests that, wherever possible, planning authorities should seek the enhancement of landscape and nature conservation within the Green Belt.

7.5. London's Green Belt is a permanent feature and should be safeguarded in plans. There is a presumption against inappropriate development in the Green Belt. PPG2 explains that such development should not be approved except in very special circumstances. The Green Belt in London has a historic significance, dating from legislation before the Second World War. Because it surrounds a very large and dense urban conurbation it is particularly vulnerable to development pressure but, if its character is to be maintained, it has only a limited scope to accept development. PPG2 (para 2.23) seeks safeguarding for future development in green belts, but in London this should be limited to specifically identified sites likely to be developed after 2006 which will not compromise the permanence or integrity of the Metropolitan Green Belt. Figure 7.1 shows major developments granted within Green Belt and MOL in recent years.

7.6. Although the boundaries of the Green Belt should be changed only in exceptional circumstances, there may be limited occasions where the loss of Green Belt is considered acceptable to achieve regeneration objectives. In these cases, all changes should be undertaken through alteration of the UDP rather than through departure procedures. These should be clearly identified and justified. The review of UDPs provides the main opportunity for each Borough to consider changes.

Where isolated pockets of Green Belt exist that are not part of a continuous pattern of open land surrounding London, authorities should consider whether it would be more appropriate to designate the land as MOL in recognition of its location and use, having regard to the guidance on MOL below.

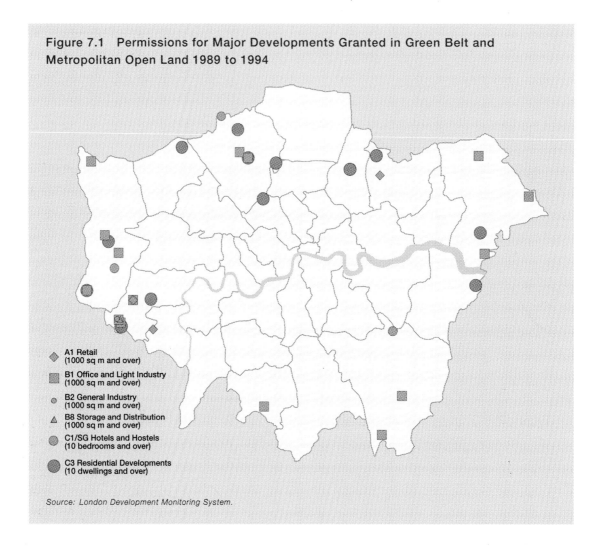

Figure 7.1 Permissions for Major Developments Granted in Green Belt and Metropolitan Open Land 1989 to 1994

◆ A1 Retail (1000 sq m and over)

■ B1 Office and Light Industry (1000 sq m and over)

◎ B2 General Industry (1000 sq m and over)

△ B8 Storage and Distribution (1000 sq m and over)

● C1/SG Hotels and Hostels (10 bedrooms and over)

● C3 Residential Developments (10 dwellings and over)

Source: London Development Monitoring System.

Metropolitan Open Land

7.7. MOL has been recognised as land of predominately open character which has more than a Borough significance, generally because of its size and catchment area. The main criteria for MOL designation are:

- land which contributes to the physical structure of London by being clearly distinguishable from the built up area

- land which includes open air facilities, especially for leisure, recreation, sport, arts and cultural activities and tourism which serve the whole or significant parts of London

- land which contains features or landscape of historic, recreational, nature conservation or habitat interest, of value at a metropolitan or national level.

7.8. Land of this importance should not be used for developments which compromise its open character and value to London's green setting. The principles of control over development in the Green Belt, set out in PPG2, also apply to MOL. There is a presumption against inappropriate development including development which would be harmful to the open character of the land. Such development should only be allowed in very special circumstances. However, as MOL encompasses a wide range of sites and locations, limited development to serve the needs of the visiting public may not be considered inappropriate development if clearly ancillary to the identified purpose of the MOL. Boroughs should assess the effects of such developments on the MOL and its environment, including the arrangements made for access by sustainable means of transport. Where proposals for other development are prepared, such as wider recreation facilities for which there is great public demand, they should be dealt with through a specific alteration to the UDP which enables all the issues to be clearly and publicly addressed.

7.9. Although MOL may vary in size and primary function across London, particularly between inner and outer London, there is a need for greater consistency between Boroughs in its designation. The designation of too small or more locally significant areas of land, for example, will devalue the strength of designation as a whole. If the land does not serve a catchment area of strategic significance or draw visitors from several Boroughs it may be more appropriate to propose and justify other local designations.

7.10. Boroughs should:

- set out strategic policies for the long term future of the Green Belt

- review the designation of MOL in consultation with neighbouring authorities and LPAC to ensure consistency of approach

- show detailed Green Belt and MOL boundaries on proposals maps, taking into account PPG2 and para 7.7 of this guidance respectively. Where it is necessary to include safeguarded land under PPG2 para 2.12, this should be made explicit

- include land use policies which support efforts to improve the nature conservation and landscape character and quality of the Green Belt and MOL

- encourage the maintenance and support of agriculture as a major economic activity in the Green Belt (reflecting the advice of PPG2 and PPG7 on retaining and protecting the best and most versatile agricultural land)

- include policies and proposals which exploit opportunities for the outdoor recreational use of the Green Belt and MOL, including increased public access where this does not conflict with

other environmental objectives

- seek to minimise conflicts and encroachment on the Green Belt and MOL near the urban fringe.

Green chains and walking routes

7.11. Green chains comprise a series of elongated undeveloped green spaces linking broader areas of open land. The pattern of open land which results helps to define parts of London, especially where the chains follow topographic features such as hills or river valleys. They may provide walking or cycling routes and permit relief from the effects of traffic. Where these chains and their associated open spaces are of more than individual Borough significance, they should be designated as MOL. Green chains might also serve as wildlife corridors which provide a network of open spaces enhancing local ecological diversity.

7.12. Longer distance walking routes in London are being implemented, mainly in outer London, through the London Walking Forum and in the Countryside Commission's Thames Path (Fig 7.2). These are characterised by green walks rather than the town trail type of walk centred on historic built areas. Such walking routes not only provide a leisure function, but contribute to achieving a sustainable transport system. Boroughs should ensure that their UDPs show proposed routes on Proposals Maps and that routes are coordinated across Borough boundaries. The London Walking Forum can provide a focus for coordination and advice on expanding the network. The Government Office for London has also undertaken a study of walking routes more appropriate for inner London, to complement the London Walking Forum's network and to achieve attractive routes through the more intensively built up parts of the capital. This study (Government Office for London 1996) has shown the scope for longer distance routes into central London. As proposals for walking routes are developed, they should be incorporated into UDPs.

Trees and green corridors

7.13. Trees and woodlands in London serve a number of purposes:

- conserving and enhancing biodiversity

- conserving and enhancing the physical environment

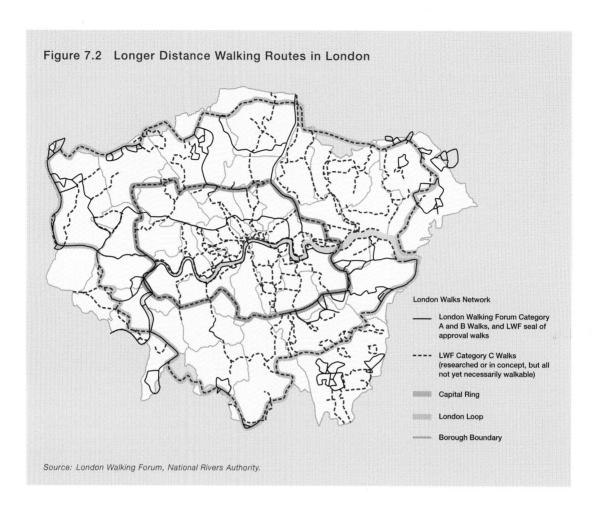

Figure 7.2   Longer Distance Walking Routes in London

London Walks Network

London Walking Forum Category
A and B Walks, and LWF seal of
approval walks

LWF Category C Walks
(researched or in concept, but all
not yet necessarily walkable)

Capital Ring

London Loop

Borough Boundary

Source: London Walking Forum, National Rivers Authority.

- maintaining air quality

- developing opportunities for recreational enjoyment

- conserving and enhancing landscape and cultural heritage.

Trees are an integral part of London's townscape and can contribute to good quality urban design. It is important that existing trees of value are protected, but, as trees age and are subject to damage, new planting should be considered for the benefit of existing and future generations. Sites for additional tree planting should be identified where they are unlikely to compromise the structural stability of buildings.

7.14.   The importance and need for trees was recognised in *Action for London's Trees*, a Countryside Commission report published in 1993 (Countryside Commission 1993).   It proposed tree planting along London's transport routes as a means of enhancing the perception of London as a leafy and pleasant city, and to create "Green Corridors" (Fig 7.3). Green

corridors can be defined as extensive contiguous areas of trees and open land which straddle the major road, rail and river/canal routes into London. A study of Green Corridors recently commissioned by GOL and the Countryside Commission demonstrates the opportunities and mechanisms by which London's principal transport routes can form Green Corridors and gateways into and out of London (GOL with Countryside Commission 1995c). It recommends that the concept should be promoted and developed through the planning system.

7.15.   Woodlands are also an important recreational resource. Epping Forest is a valuable asset to east and north London.   Thames Chase and Watling Chase Community Forests, two of the twelve Community Forests located on the fringes of major centres of population throughout England, include parts of London within their boundaries. Thames Chase covers parts of Havering and Barking and Dagenham, and extends into Essex. Watling Chase lies to the north and covers parts of Barnet, Harrow and Enfield. The Community Forests are part of a joint initiative by the Countryside Commission and

Figure 7.3 Green Corridors and Community Forests in London

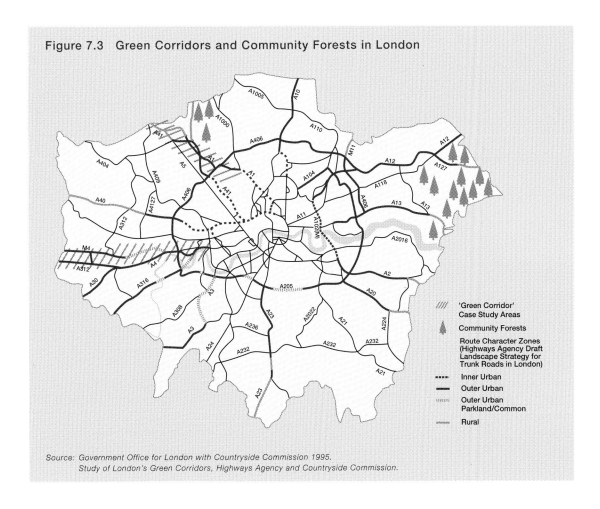

////	'Green Corridor' Case Study Areas
▲	Community Forests
	Route Character Zones (Highways Agency Draft Landscape Strategy for Trunk Roads in London)
▪▪▪▪	Inner Urban
▬▬	Outer Urban
⋯⋯⋯	Outer Urban Parkland/Common
∿∿∿	Rural

Source: Government Office for London with Countryside Commission 1995.
Study of London's Green Corridors, Highways Agency and Countryside Commission.

Forestry Commission and are intended to be a means of improving the landscape and nature conservation interests of the urban fringe, as well as creating a new recreational resource for the local population and, in future years, producing timber.

Boroughs should:

• investigate the scope for establishing walking routes and Green Chains and set out policies and proposals in UDPs in consultation with neighbouring Boroughs

• include policies and proposals for creating and implementing Green Corridors along major transport routes

• draw up policies which facilitate the establishment of the Thames Chase and Watling Chase Community Forests and include proposals for associated recreational facilities

• provide policies for the protection of trees and proposals for sites which should be used for planting.

Other open land

7.16. There are many other open spaces which are part of the urban structure but which are not large or significant enough to be designated as Green Belt or MOL. They are nevertheless valuable in providing breaks in the built-up area, providing space for recreation for residents and assisting nature conservation. Although these spaces are mainly of local significance, they make an important contribution to the image of a green and leafy city, increasing its potential ecological diversity. Examples of these include urban parks, squares, city farms, playing fields, commons, heaths, woodlands, and allotments. They contribute to a good quality of life for those who live and work in London and for visitors.

7.17. For planning purposes an appropriate definition of public open space in London is:

• public parks, commons, heaths and woodland and other open spaces with established and unrestricted public access and capable of being classified according to an open space hierarchy, though not necessarily publicly owned.

Planning for the provision of local open space is a matter for each Borough and the UDP should contain proposals for such spaces. As is made clear in PPG17, local planning authorities should identify deficiencies in public open space and recreation provision and justify the amount and location of new provision against other competing pressures for the use of land. To achieve this Boroughs should draw up their own standards for open space provision, based on the standards which were recommended in LPAC's 1994 Advice (Table 7.1).

7.18. In London there is also green space where public access is restricted or not formally established but which contributes to local amenity or meets, or is capable of meeting, recreational needs. Such spaces are valuable and Boroughs should consider whether they should be protected. In some cases public access should be negotiated: for example, when sites are subject to redevelopment proposals. Green space is particularly important in residential areas. In meeting London's housing needs (see Chapter 4), full account must be taken of the value of existing public and private open space. The proper provision of open space should be part of planning for new residential developments, especially in areas of deficiency.

7.19. Boroughs should:

- identify open space as part of a review of the UDP, where this has not already been done

- identify areas of public open space deficiencies in UDPs

- seek to reduce deficiencies in open space, either through the creation of new open space to which the public have access for enjoyment or by enabling convenient access for all to existing open space

- seek to maintain and enhance the quality of parks and other open space and aim to increase their value for both people and wildlife

- identify the contribution of other green spaces and, where appropriate, include policies for its protection.

Sport and recreation

7.20. Facilities for sport and recreation in London are required in order to improve the quality of life of those who live in the capital, as well as to contribute towards London's reputation as a world sporting city. People should have access to a range of high quality sports facilities. PPG17 sets out the Government's policy towards sport and recreation, which Boroughs should consider when assessing their own requirements. Boroughs should also consider London Sport's *The Sporting Capital: The Regional Recreation Strategy for London* (London Sport 1994). This provides a background and framework for sport in London, and an approach to achieving the vision for the future. Boroughs are unlikely to be self contained in the provision of playing fields. When assessing playing field requirements Boroughs should have regard to the accessibility of such facilities to the areas they serve. London Sport's *A Playing Fields Strategy for London* (London Sport 1990) and the Sport Council's *The Playing Pitch Strategy* (Sports Council 1991) provide an approach to local playing field provision. Given the increased demand for covered recreation facilities, sites in town centres and close to public transport should be identified to avoid pressure for development on open land and to contribute to more sustainable patterns of movement.

7.21. Development to enhance the facilities of sites of national and international importance should be encouraged. Venues include Crystal Palace, Lords, The Oval, Twickenham, Wembley Stadium and Wimbledon. New facilities may be developed as a result of Millennium, Lottery or Partnership bids. Other events take place on temporary sites or on streets, for example the London Marathon through east and central London. The Thames is the location for several events and festivities, and a Regional Regatta Centre has been established in Docklands. Boroughs should take account of the needs and location of such events as appropriate and include policies for new opportunities when they occur.

7.22. The Lee Valley Regional Park was established by the Lee Valley Regional Park Act 1966. It provides an almost continuous open space astride the River Lee stretching northwards from the River Thames in Tower Hamlets and Newham, through Hackney, Waltham Forest, Haringey and Enfield where it crosses the London boundary into Hertfordshire and Essex. This green lung is an important feature, for which the Regional Park was established to "develop, improve, preserve and manage as a place for the occupation of leisure, recreation, sport, games or amusements or any similar activity, for the provision of nature reserves and for the provision and

The Lee Valley Regional Park Authority (LVRPA) - whose composition includes representatives of local authorities within the Park boundaries - has produced a plan for the area. The latest version was adopted in 1986 and is under review. By virtue of the Lee Valley Regional Park Act 1966 local planning authorities are required to include proposals in the Park Plan in their development plans. The inclusion by a local planning authority in their development plan of any such proposal is not to be treated as indicating the approval of the local planning authority.

Within the London part of the Lee Valley most of the open space is designated either as Green Belt or MOL. Development plans reflect this and also include other designations and policies, for example to protect the nature conservation value and landscape of parts of the Park. Parts of the Lee Valley are a potential Special Protection Area for wild birds (see paragraph 7.24.). In fulfilling its statutory remit the LVRPA has provided a range of indoor and outdoor leisure and recreational facilities and undertaken substantial landscaping and land reclamation works. The 1986 Park Plan makes provision for this as do some adopted and draft development plans.

In the years since the establishment of the Authority, development has taken place in accordance with the Park Plan. While development has generally reflected Green Belt, MOL and other designations, in some instances it has taken place on land not at that time designated Green Belt or MOL. This has involved a considerable amount of building which could now be considered contrary to current national planning guidance.

Boroughs and the LVRPA should coordinate their policies when reviewing their respective plans to avoid policies and proposals which might conflict. Unless there are local circumstances which can be fully justified or other very special circumstances, UDPs should reflect prevailing national guidance, particularly PPG2. When reviewing a UDP which includes land in the Regional Park, the Borough should have regard to the Park Plan and include the Plan's proposals for the future use and development of the Park in its UDP. Where the Borough agrees with a proposal for development in the Green Belt or MOL which would otherwise be contrary to national planning guidance or this Strategic Guidance, the proposal must be clearly written as a proposal in the UDP and justified in terms of local or other very special circumstances. If the Borough does not agree to the inclusion of the Park Plan's proposal because it considers no such special circumstances apply, or for any other reason, the UDP should contain a statement setting out the Park Plan's proposal and a reasoned explanation as to why it is considered unacceptable.

enjoyments of entertainments of any kind". Boroughs should take into account the role of the Regional Park Authority in the provision of leisure and recreation facilities.

Nature conservation

7.23. Boroughs should have regard to the national policies on nature conservation and development planning set out in PPG9. UDPs should reflect the fact that nature conservation objectives should be taken into account in all planning activities which affect rural land use and in urban areas where there is local nature conservation interest. Boroughs should draw up policies and proposals for the protection and enhancement of sites of metropolitan, national and international importance.

7.24. Sites with national and international designations, such as Sites of Special Scientific Interest (SSSIs), National Nature Reserves (NNRs), Special Protection Areas (SPAs), Special Areas of Conservation (SACs) and Ramsar sites, should be identified in UDPs to establish a strategic framework for nature conservation. (Map 8). SPAs and SACs are intended to protect habitats of threatened species of wildlife. Ramsar sites are listed by the Secretary of State to protect wetlands that are of international importance, particularly as waterfowl habitats. In and around London, potential SPAs include the Lee Valley and the south west London Reservoirs and Gravel Pits (now known as South West London Waterbodies). Annex A of PPG9 explains these designations in more detail. The framework should also include Sites of Metropolitan Importance, as identified by the London Ecology Unit, which may also be of national importance. All these sites should be shown on the Proposals Map.

7.25. Local nature conservation interests should also be taken into account. UDPs should include policies for the conservation of the natural beauty and amenity of the land. Boroughs should also consider the value of creating new nature conservation areas. The London Ecology Unit hierarchy (LPAC 1995a) provides a basis for this approach. Boroughs should refer to English Nature's document *Planning for Wildlife in Towns and Cities* (English Nature 1994) and the Ecology Handbooks published by the London Ecology Unit (London Ecology Unit 1984 onwards).

space and cremation in convenient and accessible locations. This should be achieved without encroaching upon existing sport or open air recreation facilities, areas of importance for nature conservation or buildings and features of architectural or historical interest.

Burial space

7.26. Boroughs, when reviewing UDPs and in cooperation with each other, should make provision, wherever possible, to meet the demand for burial

Table 7.1: Types of Publicly Accessible Open Space in London

Type and Main Function	Approx. Size and Distance from Home	Characteristics
REGIONAL PARKS AND OPEN SPACE (Linked Metropolitan Open Land and Green Belt Corridors) Weekend and occasional visits by car or public transport	400 hectares 3.2-8 km	Large areas and corridors of natural heathland, downland, commons, woodlands and parkland also including areas not publicly accessible but which contribute to the overall environmental amenity. Primarily providing for informal recreation with some non-intensive active recreation uses. Car parking at key locations.
METROPOLITAN PARKS Weekend and occasional visits by car or public transport	60 hectares 3.2 km or more where the park is appreciably larger	Either i. natural heathland, downland, commons, woodlands etc. or ii. formal parks providing for both active and passive recreation. May contain playing fields, but at least 40 hectares for other pursuits. Adequate car parking.
DISTRICT PARKS Weekend and occasional visits by foot, cycle, car and short bus trips	20 hectares 1.2 km	Landscape setting with a variety of natural features providing for a wide range of activities, including outdoor sports facilities and playing fields, children's play for different age groups, and informal recreation pursuits. Should provide some car parking.
LOCAL PARKS Pedestrian visits	2 hectares 0.4 km	Providing for court games, children's play, sitting-out areas, nature conservation areas.
SMALL LOCAL PARKS AND OPEN SPACES Pedestrian visits, especially by old people and children; particularly valuable in high density areas.	under 2 hectares less than 0.4 km	Gardens, sitting-out areas, children's play spaces or other areas of a specialist nature, including nature conservation areas.
LINEAR OPEN SPACES Pedestrian visits	Variable; wherever feasible.	The Thames, canals, other waterways and associated open spaces and towpaths; paths; disused railways; nature conservation areas; and other routes which provide opportunities for informal recreation. Often characterised by features or attractive areas which are not fully accessible to the public but contribute to the enjoyment of the space.

Source: LPAC 1994a.

Map 7 Green Belt and Metropolitan Open Land

Green Belt

Metropolitan Open Land

This map gives a general indication of the extent of both adopted and proprosed Green Belt and Metropolitan Open Land in London. Information on detailed boundaries may be obtained from local planning authorities.

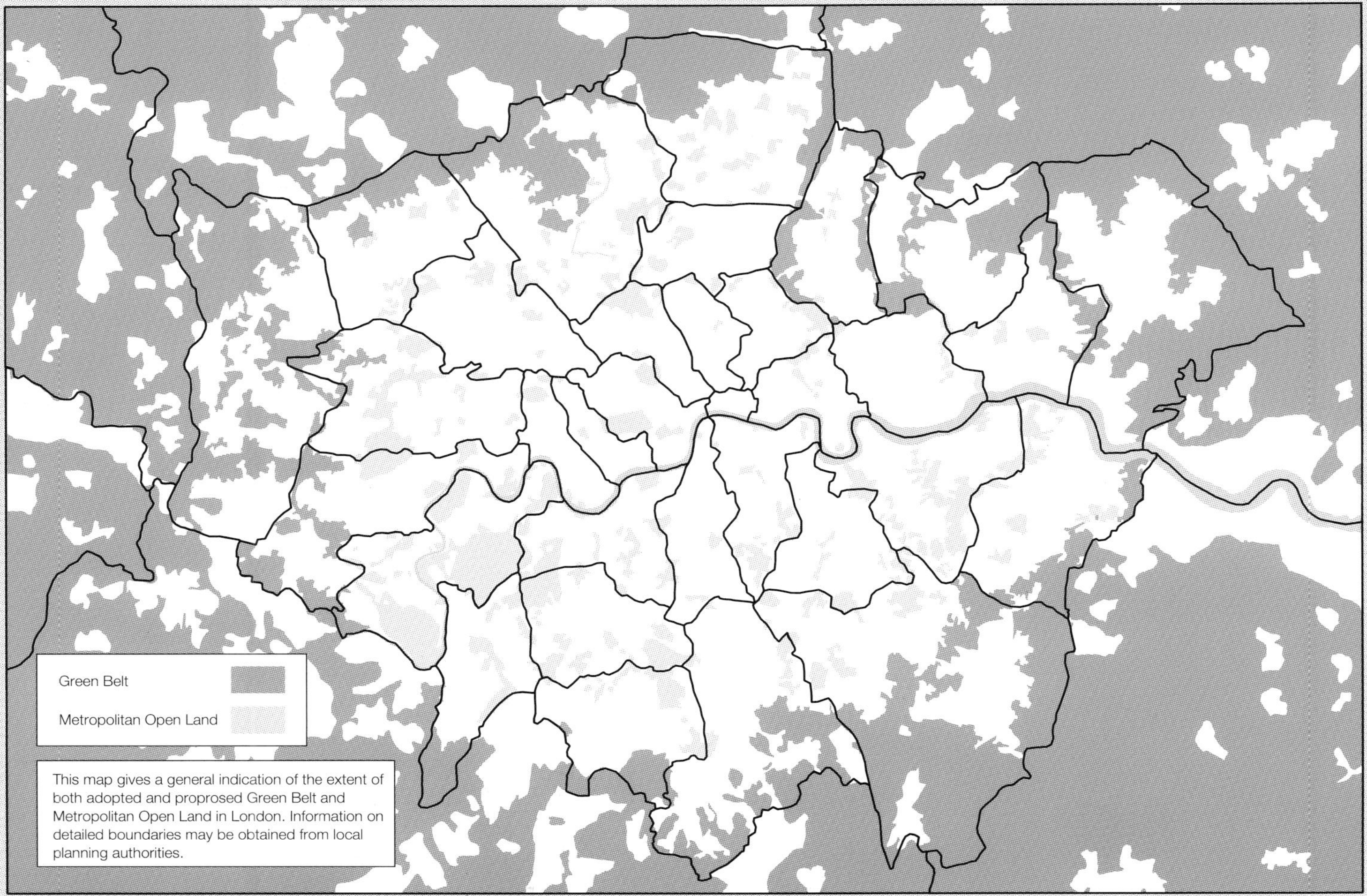

Map 8   Conservation

This map gives a general indication of the extent of Environmental Designations in London shown in Borough UDPs. Information on detailed boundaries may be obtained from local planning authorities. Information used to compile map provided by LUC from English Heritage/LPAC Conservation in London Study, 1995.

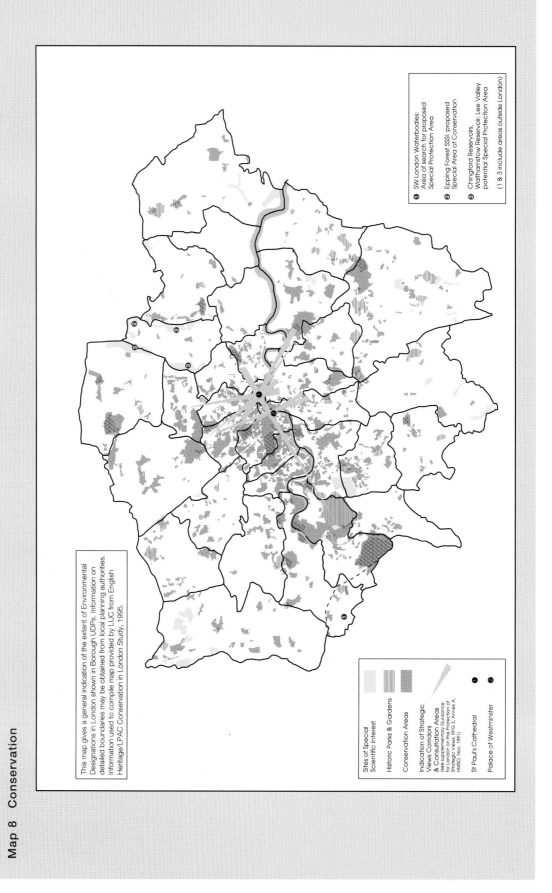

① SW London Waterbodies:
Area of search for proposed
Special Protection Area

② Epping Forest SSSI: proposed
Special Area of Conservation

③ Chingford Reservoirs,
Walthamstow Reservoir: Lee Valley
potential Special Protection Area

(1 & 3 include areas outside London)

Sites of Special
Scientific Interest

Historic Parks & Gardens

Conservation Areas

Indication of Strategic
Views Corridors
& Consultation Areas
(see supplementary Guidance
for London on the Protection of
Strategic Views, RPG 3, Annex A,
HMSO, Nov. 1991)

● St Paul's Cathedral

◉ Palace of Westminster

8. The Built and Historic Environment

8.1. The quality and character of London's urban environment is a major asset highly valued by those who live, work, visit and invest in the capital. It is essential to protect and improve the quality of the environment in order to maintain London's attractiveness and competitiveness.

Urban quality goals and components

8.2. Good design and a high quality environment should be the aim of all those involved in development. The planning system has a pivotal role in helping to promote and implement measures which help to preserve, complement or enhance the quality of the urban environment. The Department of the Environment discussion document *Quality in Town and Country* (Department of the Environment 1994d) and the subsequent Urban Design Campaign (Department of the Environment 1995d) recognise that promoting quality is something which affects us all, promotes sustainability and makes good economic sense.

8.3. Research undertaken for the Department of the Environment and LPAC (LPAC 1994f) has shown that increased environmental quality has an accepted social and environmental value and that it can be recognised and implemented at a variety of levels from the very detailed to the strategic. The Government has itself set in hand initiatives including developing planning principles for the Thames Gateway and the Thames, which give specific guidance in these areas. Further guidance will be given in the revision of PPG1, expected to be published in 1996.

8.4. In addition further research was commissioned by GOL to identify goals for urban quality in London which those involved in planning for, developing and maintaining the environment could recognise (Government Office for London 1996b). The report has shown that it is possible to identify key themes which should underpin Borough planning activity.

8.5. There is no single or simple answer to achieving an improved quality of built environment. Each area or site will present a different context and opportunity. In some locations it may be sensible to protect the existing environment as far as possible.

> **Suggested Goals for Promoting Urban Quality in London**
>
> **A city that is or has:**
>
> - well designed and visually rich
> - quality open space
> - distinctive place and identity
> - human scale skyline and wonderful views
> - a rich mix of uses and diversity of attractions
> - ease of accessibility for all
> - high amenity value especially in its heritage areas
> - pedestrian friendly environments and transport corridors
> - safe and sustainable environments, especially in residential areas
> - well managed and maintained throughout.
>
> *Source: Government Office for London 1996b.*

Other locations may require or offer the opportunity for a bold new response. The identification of a number of "core components" will help to achieve an improved quality of the built environment through a better ability to understand the urban environment, the need for change and the effect of different proposals (Fig 8.1). The understanding of these issues and assessment of proposals against them should be an important part of development planning activity in London. The articulation of core components should make proposals easier to understand by the public and may assist in the environmental appraisal of policies.

8.6. Boroughs should:

- set out strategic policies which incorporate the goals of urban quality identified above and encourage well designed development that both respects the character of its locality and adds to the quality of the wider environment

- promote improvements to the visual environment

- give particular consideration to specific initiatives, or proposals for areas which can achieve improvements of quality

- justify policies and the areas in which they will apply in terms of the character of the area, if necessary undertaking an initial character assessment of the Borough

- take a flexible approach towards new or alternative uses particularly in areas where

buildings are vacant, under-used or the environment is deteriorating and where regeneration is an important objective

- ensure that policies are realistic, not prescriptive or over-restrictive and consider them against the core components of urban quality illustrated here.

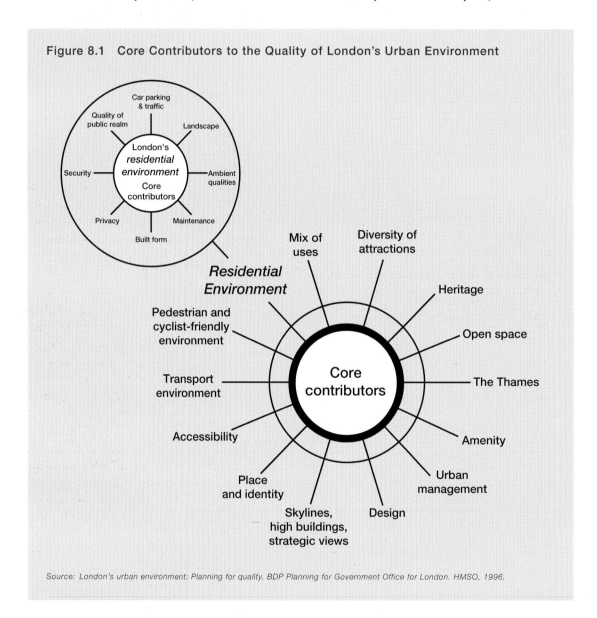

Figure 8.1   Core Contributors to the Quality of London's Urban Environment

Source: London's urban environment: Planning for quality. BDP Planning for Government Office for London. HMSO, 1996.

Conservation

8.7.   London contains many of the country's most famous buildings, districts and landmarks. These buildings and areas contribute to London's diversity and vitality and include Conservation Areas; Historic Parks and Gardens included in the English Heritage Register; World Heritage Sites; Areas of Archaeological Significance; Ancient Monuments; Listed Buildings, and London Squares (Map 8). They are important as a focus for tourism as well as for

their intrinsic interest. The Government's policies concerning planning for such areas and for buildings of special architectural and historic importance and archaeology are set out in PPG15 and PPG16. The Secretary of State has also had regard to the English Heritage/LPAC report on Conservation in London (English Heritage with LPAC 1995), and supports the overall recommendations to promote the viable use of buildings at risk and the use of conservation objectives as a focus for urban regeneration where feasible.

8.8. Boroughs should:

- identify appropriate areas, spaces and buildings of special quality or character, including conservation areas

- promote policies for the conservation of areas and buildings which complement the appropriate designation of areas

- include policies for the re-use of redundant historic buildings and recognise where conservation initiatives can aid urban regeneration and vice versa.

8.9. Boroughs should also take account of the desirability of recognising and preserving the ancient historic environment and remains. UDPs should carry forward the advice in PPG16 on the protection of nationally important archaeological remains and their settings. In the case of remains of lesser importance, policies should seek to balance the preservation and recording of remains against the need for development.

Residential quality

8.10. In view of the concern about the importance of making the fullest use of urban land and to avoid urban sprawl and unsustainable patterns of living, it is important that residential areas strike a balance between the provision of adequate housing and the preservation and enhancement of the environment. The UDP should reflect the existing pattern of development in the Borough and plan for future needs. Policies should be reviewed in the light of strategic and regional policies to concentrate development in existing urban areas. In London, the existence of a continuous built up area served by good infrastructure suggests that there are opportunities for making better use of existing resources and for improving quality especially in areas where selective renewal can be facilitated.

8.11. The standards of housing density appropriate in different localities in London vary widely. Density policies have often been important in setting the pattern of development, particularly in encouraging the dispersal of population, the layout of new neighbourhoods and the reconstruction of bomb-damaged areas after the war. Although the Secretary of State does not consider that it would be helpful to set a London-wide density guideline in formal guidance, Boroughs should reassess the density assumptions they are using with a view to encouraging higher densities where appropriate in the light of the guidance given in this Chapter and in Chapter 4.

8.12. There are opportunities in London for a wide range of densities, linked to the provision of different types of housing. The Secretary of State considers that the next review of UDPs should be the occasion for each Borough to examine the scope for raising densities. Locations which merit consideration for higher densities include those in or close to existing centres and public transport nodes or where new or converted properties are being developed to meet the needs of smaller households. Areas with larger than average concentrations of houses in multiple occupation, student accommodation and hostels will also be suitable for higher densities. At the same time, London should attract those seeking family housing and who desire more spacious surroundings, so a range of densities should be offered on large sites.

8.13. Higher densities and a more economical use of space can be achieved through better attention to design. Boroughs have an opportunity to contribute to this through good site planning and the preparation of briefs for developers, and clear straightforward policies on standards and layout. In this way the problems typified by the term "town cramming" can be avoided. The application of development control standards should facilitate the creation of buildings and places of high quality. Care must be taken not to thwart innovative designs and layouts, particularly those sensitive to their content, by an inflexible application of standards. The standards themselves should be kept under review. Decisions on housing layout should also take account of the role of public and private open land in securing a good quality urban environment. While each application has to be considered on its merits, the UDP provides the opportunity to set out guidance on the relationship between the application and other land uses. This will become increasingly important if the challenge of mixed uses is to be satisfactorily met.

8.14. Examples of factors that should be considered include:

- the balance of residential types and densities on sites in the same locality

- the relationship between residential uses and other uses, especially local shops and services, to increase proximity but avoid nuisance

- the relationship between private and public open space (in urban environments, the provision of good publicly accessible open space needs to be considered against the desirability of private and defensible space.)

- the economical use of circulation and parking space serving the development

- the opportunity to enhance the street scene by such measures as planting, the removal of clutter, rationalisation of signs and improved street furniture

- the opportunity to use high densities where appropriate to enhance the visual quality and diversity of the street scene

- the need to ensure that residents have access to community facilities, for example primary health care, education and places of worship.

8.15.   Traffic management and calming can do much to ameliorate the difficulties caused by demands for space for parking and vehicular movement and the pressure for loss of gardens and vegetation to create hard standings for vehicles. In some cases, particularly in outer London, more road space could be made available for parking near to the dwelling, reducing the need for parking within the curtilage. In addition, over the years of this Guidance, it is likely that changes will occur in the weight given to the need to provide urban space for the car. More sustainable patterns of development, good public transport and concerns over air quality make it increasingly probable that the historic link between income, car ownership and car use will be re-evaluated. It is therefore important that Boroughs provide the opportunity for a choice of lifestyles and do not inhibit innovation by inflexible standards. For example, car free housing schemes are being developed in Europe and the UK. Designs which offer enhanced quality close to public transport, walking and cycling in exchange for the space occupied by the car are expected to find a growing market, particularly in inner areas accessible to good local facilities.

8.16.   Some of the most acute difficulties occur in streets where conversion activity would be desirable to increase housing stock, but where existing residents fear that their amenities will be compromised by the intensification which conversion may represent. Boroughs should not seek a blanket restriction against conversions over wide parts of their area but may identify areas suitable or unsuitable for conversion activity. Areas which merit a restrictive approach will need to be defined clearly and fully justified within UDPs. Standards should not be applied in a prescriptive manner but Boroughs may consider identifying criteria to encourage a good quality of development. In particular, parking standards should not be used unnecessarily to restrict the supply of conversions, especially where the location is well served by public transport. Boroughs which wish to have generous minimum parking standards in such areas will need to give a full and adequate reasoning as to why such standards are deemed to be necessary. Recent research for the Department of the Environment has indicated that the demand for parking from a house that has been converted is often no more than from a similar single dwelling house, where a larger single household may own several cars (LPAC 1994f). Although in the short term occupants' aspirations to own and use cars may well rise as their incomes increase or family status changes, in the longer term there is an opportunity to improve local environments by restricting parking provision from the outset and relying more on sustainable means of transport.

8.17.   Boroughs where appropriate should:

- revise preferred residential densities, having regard to economy in the use of land, sustainability and the quality of the urban environment

- review development control standards and apply these sensitively and realistically to new developments and residential conversion

- set policies allowing for a choice of lifestyles including, where demand is likely to exist, reduced car or car free areas

- identify areas most suitable for residential conversions

- identify and justify areas unsuitable for residential conversions

- set out policies and criteria against which

applications for conversions will be determined in areas not specifically identified.

Important views and high buildings

8.18. It is important to consider the three dimensional nature of the built environment and to give careful consideration to the location of high buildings. Supplementary Guidance on the protection of ten strategic views of St Paul's Cathedral and the Palace of Westminster was published as an annex to RPG3 in November 1991. Separate Directions were issued under the Town and Country Planning General Development Order 1988 to help protect each view from inappropriate development. Such views will normally cross several Boroughs. The annex will remain in force until replaced by a revised document to be published after this Guidance which may consider the merits of designating additional views. Boroughs should exercise their development control responsibilities to enhance the views where possible.

8.19. In addition to including appropriate policies to protect existing strategic views, Boroughs should consider the need to protect important local views including those which encompass historic and notable buildings and vistas. This should be undertaken in the light of criteria for the location of such views linked to a clear methodology for their protection. Where local views cross Borough boundaries, neighbouring Boroughs should cooperate and consult to ensure that there is a consistent approach on policies and proposals in UDPs.

8.20. In determining planning applications, Boroughs should give careful consideration to the height, density, scale, massing, bulk, landscaping, design and architectural quality of proposed buildings, having regard to the existing character of the area. In consultation with neighbouring authorities and LPAC, clear definitions should be given for the heights of buildings which may require particular assessments in different parts of the Borough. It may be appropriate to define areas which are either unsuitable or particularly suitable for high buildings. In some locations, a high building may be appropriate but only if of an exceptional quality of design to create a prominent feature of the townscape. Such areas and policies would need to be especially well justified and should demonstrate how the designation of such areas relates to wider and specific conservation, quality and townscape policies and proposals.

8.21. Specific account will need to be taken in appropriate locations of the requirement for public safety and consultation zones near airports. These should be shown in UDPs. Plans should also take account of zones where development is affected by microwave communication corridors. Further information is given in PPG8.

8.22. Boroughs should:

- include appropriate policies in UDPs to protect and enhance existing strategic views

- protect important local views, by showing them on the Proposals Map after consultation with neighbouring Boroughs in those cases where the view crosses Borough boundaries

- identify areas considered particularly appropriate or inappropriate for high buildings

- include safeguarding areas near airports and in telecommunication corridors.

9. Waste, Pollution, Minerals, Water and Energy

INTRODUCTION

9.1.   A large city generates considerable waste from its everyday activities, while pollution can occur from its use of energy and demands for industry and transport. Increasing concern about the quality of the environment and the necessity to develop a more sustainable economy means that efforts to reduce the production of waste and pollutants at source should be continued . Opportunities to re-use and recycle waste materials should be exploited. Land use planning can make a contribution to these aims by discouraging unacceptable development and guiding that which is acceptable to the most appropriate locations.

9.2.   Cities use considerable amounts of minerals directly or indirectly, for example in buildings and roads and in the everyday purchases of products by the community. Large quantities of water and energy are also consumed with consequent arisings of sewage and the products of energy consumption, most of which are pollutants. The planning system has an important role to play in the development and management of this consumption.

9.3.   The review of UDPs provides an opportunity to consider the planning implications of these and related issues in greater depth than was possible in many of the first round of plans. This review must include the relationship of each authority to its surroundings. As London is heavily dependent on surrounding counties and more distant locations for its growing demand for aggregates and minerals, transport and distribution aspects of supply are particularly important. The disposal of waste must be seen in the wider regional context, particularly as landfill is the major disposal route, the capacity of existing landfill void space is being used up and greater difficulties may be encountered in finding new sites.

9.4.   Under the provisions of the 1995 Environment Act, the organisations responsible for the management and regulation of waste, pollution control, water resources, water conservation and related matters - the London Waste Regulation

Authority (LWRA), Her Majesty's Inspectorate of Pollution (HMIP) and the National Rivers Authority (NRA) - have had their functions transferred to the Environment Agency which was constituted in August 1995 and which began to function on 1 April 1996. The Environment Agency (EA) has a regional structure and London is part of the Thames Region. This guidance refers to the organisation existing in 1995 but should be taken to refer to the responsibilities of the Agency.

WASTE

9.5.   In 1993/94 London produced about 12.3 million tonnes of commercial, industrial and household waste of which about three quarters was disposed to landfill. The majority of landfill takes place in surrounding counties with only about 1 million tonnes per year within London. About 0.9 million tonnes of waste is incinerated in London each year (LWRA 1995). London therefore currently relies very heavily on the movement of its waste to other parts of the South East for disposal (Figs 9.1 and 9.2). Forward planning of London's waste management must therefore take place within a regional framework.

9.6.   In accordance with the principles of sustainable development, the Government has set out a waste strategy in the White Paper *Making Waste Work* (HM Government 1995c). This sets out a hierarchy of waste management options:

* reduction

* re-use

* recovery, including recycling, composting and energy recovery

* disposal.

9.7.   Most waste is at present disposed of in landfill and is therefore at the bottom of the hierarchy. This is not sustainable in the long term and the strategy provides for greater emphasis on moving waste up the hierarchy. It also sets targets for the reduction and different treatment options for various types of waste within a given number of years. These considerations are particularly important in London where the landfill option will soon become even less sustainable as available void space in surrounding counties becomes increasingly scarce (see below).

9.8. The strategy subscribes to the "best practicable environmental option" (BPEO) procedure which establishes, for a given set of objectives, the option that provides the most benefits or least damage to the environment as a whole at an acceptable cost in the long and short term. It also subscribes to the "proximity principle" under which, taking into account BPEO, waste should be disposed of or managed close to the point at which it is generated.

9.9. In addition to the strategy in the White Paper, consideration should also be given to the national guidance in PPG23 and MPG7. Additional guidance will be provided in a PPG note on Waste Management Planning which is intended to be published by the end of 1996. It will also be important for Boroughs to work closely with the Environment Agency which will begin a national waste survey in 1996. This will help to inform the preparation of a statutory waste strategy by the Secretary of State under section 44A of the Environment Protection Act 1990 (inserted by section 92 of the Environment Act 1995). This strategy will give guidance on waste management policy and will replace the LWRA waste disposal plan. In the meantime, the existing LWRA plan and other guidance to which this chapter refers should be taken into account. The Secretary of State welcomes the studies LPAC, SERPLAN and the South East Waste Regulation Advisory Committee (SEWRAC) undertake and endorses SERPLAN's objective that the South East should aim to make adequate provision within the region for the disposal of its own waste. The aims and objectives of SERPLAN's 1992 and 1994 waste planning guidance papers (SERPLAN 1992, 1994) are relevant to planning in London.

9.10. Many of the landfill sites taking London's waste have become available elsewhere in the South East as a result of mineral working, mainly clay extraction for brick manufacture, and sand and gravel sites. Although landfill in neighbouring counties is likely to remain the primary waste disposal method in the immediate future, if recent trends continue and void space is filled faster than it is created the surplus space could be exhausted by early next century. Mineral working in the South East over the period to 2006 is not expected to take place at rates significantly different from those of recent years. Because of long lead times in the planning, development and operation of most waste management and disposal facilities authorities should already be investigating and planning alternative methods of waste management. As the availability of disposal sites and methods of waste treatment and final disposal change, there are likely to be both economic and environmental consequences and these will need to be taken into account. When drawing up policies for waste management including disposal in their UDPs, Boroughs should have regard, in addition to SERPLAN's guidance, to the LWRA's waste management plan (LWRA 1995). This deals with such matters as waste generation, types and quantities, handling and treatment, transport, site operating criteria and licensing.

9.11. Boroughs should reflect the Government's views on the waste hierarchy in policies for the reduction of waste generation and the encouragement of recycling and energy recovery in their UDPs. In particular the potential for recycling household waste, the amount of which is currently minimal in most parts of London, should be exploited. Boroughs will therefore need to consider:

• the urban design implications of new forms of kerbside collections

• the siting and design of collection points for household wastes

• the need for recycling and energy recovery plant (including combined heat and power) in their areas

• the need for incineration plant and waste transfer/bulk reducing stations in their areas.

Disposal methods should reflect an acceptable balance locally and for London as a whole, paying regard to economics, land use and the environment, the effects on the potential for development in the area and the use of different modes of transport for the movement of wastes and residues. Boroughs should cooperate and work collectively, particularly with their neighbours, with LPAC, SERPLAN, the EA and with the waste disposal industry, to provide an acceptable comprehensive policy framework for the disposal of London's waste.

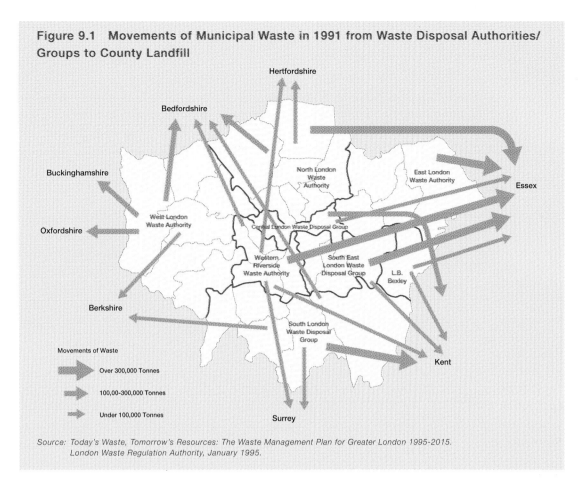

Figure 9.1 Movements of Municipal Waste in 1991 from Waste Disposal Authorities/ Groups to County Landfill

Source: *Today's Waste, Tomorrow's Resources: The Waste Management Plan for Greater London 1995-2015.
London Waste Regulation Authority, January 1995.*

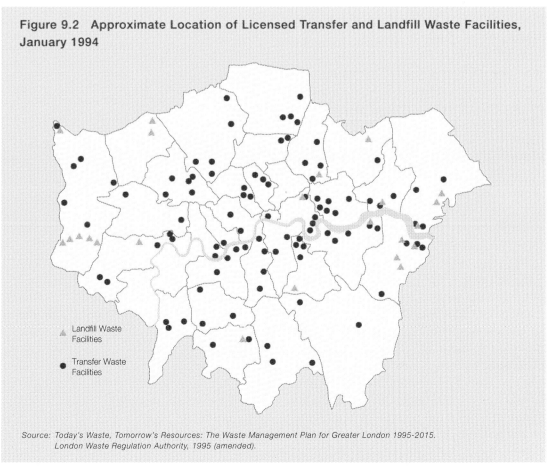

Figure 9.2 Approximate Location of Licensed Transfer and Landfill Waste Facilities, January 1994

Source: *Today's Waste, Tomorrow's Resources: The Waste Management Plan for Greater London 1995-2015.
London Waste Regulation Authority, 1995 (amended).*

9.12.   Alternative or additional provision may need to be made for:

- sewage sludge currently disposed of at sea, where this method of disposal must end in 1998

- hospital waste, which will no longer be able to be disposed of in plants unable to meet modern environmental standards

- green waste, separated from other waste and which is suitable for composting.

9.13.   Boroughs should:

- include strategic policies for the achievement of the hierarchy of waste management options, and for the anticipated provision of recycling collection points, treatment plants and transfer stations

- demonstrate that account has been taken of the potential to reduce, reuse and recycle waste in their area

- set out policies for waste reduction and minimisation at source

- set out policies and proposals for waste and refuse storage, transfer, initial treatment and disposal

- include policies and proposals for recycling and energy recovery plant (including combined heat and power), incineration plant and waste transfer/bulk reducing stations

- consider, with the aim of minimising environmental impact, the modes and routes to be used for the transport of waste, including any residues from treatment and processing, and the distribution of facilities and collection points to reduce travel

- make policies and proposals for recycling facilities, including local collection facilities (such as bottle banks and paper banks), larger comprehensive sites handling a wide range of waste materials and sites for the handling of green waste

- demonstrate that consideration has been given to the storage, treatment and disposal of specialised waste.

Where appropriate, UDPs should identify areas of search and/or specific sites which would accommodate waste recycling, transfer, disposal (including incineration) and any other facilities required. UDPs should demonstrate that liaison has taken place and that mutually acceptable and workable arrangements for waste transfer and disposal exist between originating and recipient authorities both within London and in the rest of the South East.

9.14.   If it is not considered possible or necessary to identify sites and areas with potential for development in addition to the existing main sites, the UDP should provide a full and adequate justification of the Borough's approach having had regard to the LWRA waste management plan, SERPLAN's guidance, the policies of other London Boroughs and relevant counties and site or environmental constraints. Whether or not sites have been identified, UDPs should set out criteria against which proposals for such facilities would be assessed. These should include locational considerations, access and mode of transport, transport routes, site design, appearance and layout, environmental constraints, potential effects on groundwater, mitigating measures to minimise unavoidable adverse environmental impacts (where these are likely to be under planning control) and, where appropriate, improvement in amenity. The EA should be consulted on proposals involving the use of land for the deposit of refuse or waste.

9.15.   Boroughs should consider storage compounds and scrapyards, composting and digesting plant, bulk reduction by compaction or incineration, energy recovery, combined heat and power generation and the final disposal of resultant waste. Plans should address these matters comprehensively in a similar way to that set out for recycling above. It will be particularly important to justify fully the policies proposed on incineration and final disposal, especially locational and transport considerations, having regard to the waste disposal requirements of London as a whole and the South East region. Authorities should plan for a balanced pattern of facilities and transport arrangements. In recognition of the "proximity principle" and BPEO, treatment should be undertaken locally where practicable and cost effective and transport distances should be kept to a minimum. Subject to this and satisfactory disposal options and in view of the considerable environmental benefits overall, there

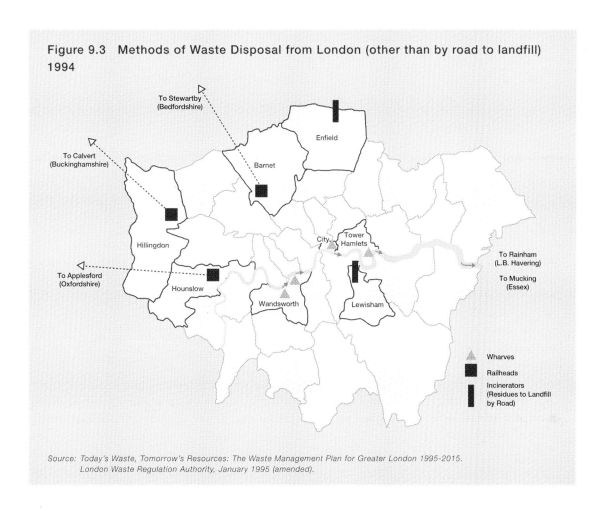

Figure 9.3 Methods of Waste Disposal from London (other than by road to landfill) 1994

To Stewartby (Bedfordshire)

To Calvert (Buckinghamshire)

To Applesford (Oxfordshire)

Enfield

Barnet

Hillingdon

City

Tower Hamlets

To Rainham (L.B. Havering)

To Mucking (Essex)

Hounslow

Wandsworth

Lewisham

Wharves

Railheads

Incinerators (Residues to Landfill by Road)

Source: Today's Waste, Tomorrow's Resources: The Waste Management Plan for Greater London 1995-2015. London Waste Regulation Authority, January 1995 (amended).

should be a presumption in favour of the movement of significant amounts of waste by rail or water. Figure 9.3 indicates existing methods of disposal of London's waste by modes of transport other than road.

9.16. Future UDPs should reflect the increased interest in the provision of local facilities and take account of their distribution in relation to residents and other main users (Fig 9.4). Licensed civic amenity sites and collection/recycling points need to be provided in such a manner as to minimise nuisance, facilitate access for collection vehicles and encourage users to minimise travel to them. Boroughs should demonstrate an understanding of the locational aspects of waste collection, disposal and recycling and integrate the provision of facilities into land use planning at the local level. The Secretary of State considers that Boroughs should not attempt to prohibit developments from their areas but should work with local communities to ensure amenity is safeguarded.

9.17. Suitable water or riverside sites should be identified and safeguarded for waste recycling, treatment and transfer facilities. Criteria should be

set out for the development of such sites. Particular attention should be paid to a high standard of design and appearance, the opportunities for enhancement and improvement of the river frontage (for example by careful use of materials, means of enclosure and landscaping) and protection of the water environment from pollution. These environmental considerations apply particularly in localities which have a run-down appearance and where land is ripe for redevelopment. Plans should include a statement of what steps have been taken to accomplish this and, where applicable, an explanation of the absence of identified sites. Existing facilities should be safeguarded. Strategic Planning Guidance for the Thames, to be published separately, will address the potential for the transport of freight by water and safeguarding issues.

9.18. The Secretary of State requests LPAC to cooperate with the Boroughs, SERPLAN, the EA and the waste management industry to report regularly on the results of studies into the reduction, recycling, treatment and disposal of waste. The need for additional guidance will be considered in the light of these studies.

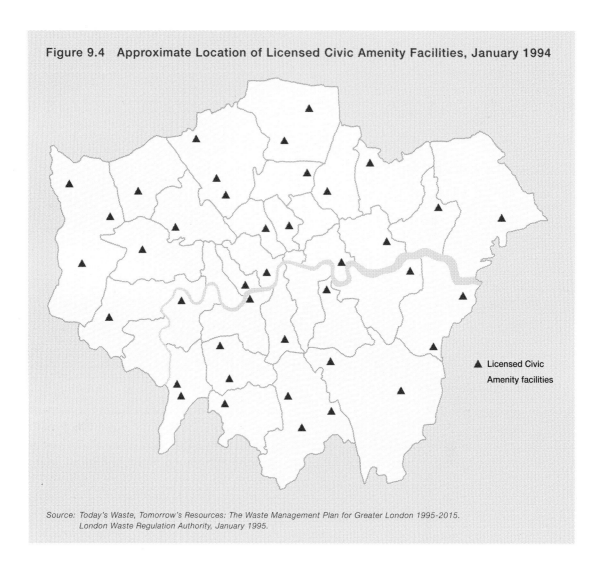

Figure 9.4   Approximate Location of Licensed Civic Amenity Facilities, January 1994

▲ Licensed Civic
   Amenity facilities

Source: Today's Waste, Tomorrow's Resources: The Waste Management Plan for Greater London 1995-2015.
London Waste Regulation Authority, January 1995.

POLLUTION

Air and land pollution

9.19.   London's economic base has changed
significantly over the years, and heavy manufacturing
and polluting industries have declined considerably.
This and the introduction of pollution controls have
led to cleaner waterways, the banishment of smog
and reduced levels of lead emissions. Airborne lead
concentrations in London have fallen to less than
one fifth of the 1983 level following the reduction
in the amount of lead allowed in petrol in 1986.
Nevertheless potentially polluting activities are
expected to continue to take place, including some
industrial and manufacturing processes, waste
treatment and disposal and combined heat and
power production. In addition, the use of energy
for heating, lighting and as a power source directly
or indirectly causes pollution through emissions of
carbon dioxide.

9.20.   The Environment Act 1995 (Part IV)
introduces a new framework for tackling air pollution
at national and local levels. Boroughs will need to
take into account the planning and transport
implications of the Act and the National Air Quality
Strategy. Land use policies should help to avoid the
concentration of different polluting activities from
different sources and should encourage sustainable
practice and development to reduce pollution. The
levels of pollution will be an important consideration
when conducting environmental appraisals of plans.
Well justified criteria against which proposals for
potentially polluting development would be assessed
will assist in the appraisal of such proposals. Further
guidance is given in PPG23.

9.21.   Exhaust emissions from vehicles are a
significant cause of air pollution. For example, some
three quarters of emissions of oxides of nitrogen in
London are from road transport (Figs 9.5 and 9.6).
It is expected that stricter controls on vehicle
emissions and, over the longer term, the continued

Air Quality

Part IV of the Environment Act 1995 provides a national and local framework for tackling air pollution. Under the Act, the Secretary of State will publish a National Air Quality Strategy which will provide a framework of standards and objectives for pollutants of most concern, including small particles. It will also include a timetable for achieving the objectives and steps the Government is taking and measures it expects others to take to see that objectives are met.

Locally there is to be a system of local air quality management in which local authorities will have a duty to carry out regular reviews of present and likely future air quality. If standards and objectives are not being met, or are unlikely to be met, within a period specified in regulations or the National Strategy, the local authority will be required to designate an Air Quality Management Area (AQMA). It will then be necessary for the authority to prepare an assessment of the air quality in the AQMA and an Air Quality Action Plan of measures to be taken within a timetable for implementation to ensure the achievement of standards and objectives within the designated AQMA.

The London Emissions Inventory is being maintained by the London Research Centre. It will be a useful source of information for local planning.

Source: The Environment Act 1995.

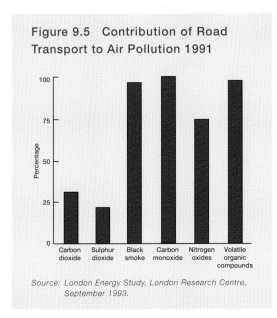

Figure 9.5 Contribution of Road Transport to Air Pollution 1991

Source: London Energy Study, London Research Centre, September 1993.

introduction of catalytic converters will secure some improvements but these may be tempered by increased traffic growth. Policies to encourage the use of public transport, walking and cycling, to reduce the need to travel and to remove through traffic from residential and shopping areas will make an important contribution to ensuring that air quality standards and objectives are met.

9.22. Tighter emission standards and improved technology will lead to a reduction in harmful emissions per vehicle while the implementation of planning policies should encourage greater use of modes of travel other than the private car. However in many areas of London traffic levels will still mean

that emissions of pollutants may continue to be undesirably high. Prescribed air quality standards may be breached, either on a regular or an occasional basis. A noxious mixture of potentially harmful pollutants may result, particularly under certain weather conditions and where pollutants are also being emitted from other sources. Traffic management measures may then have to be taken to help meet the prescribed standards. Schedule 22 of the Environment Act 1995 amends the Road Traffic Regulation Act 1984 to allow traffic regulation orders to be made on air quality management grounds. The review of UDPs will be an opportunity to consider for the longer term how transport and land use planning can be used in the interests of air quality.

9.23. A further source of pollution is ground contamination resulting from activities such as gas manufacture, industrial processes using hazardous substances, landfill with waste and sewage disposal. As many sites are likely to be capable of further development, UDPs should address issues such as the investigation required prior to development and the controls which should be imposed if development is to become acceptable at known or potentially polluted sites. Guidance in PPG23 should be taken into account.

9.24. Policies and proposals should aim to prevent encroachment by development, for example housing, on sites next to industrial processes if such development cannot reasonably co-exist with the process that has been authorised or licensed under pollution control legislation. This applies particularly where such encroachment may lead to otherwise unreasonable imposition of higher standards, refusal of a licence or closure of the business, or where the likely expansion or intensification of the use (assuming that this would be otherwise acceptable on planning grounds) would be prejudiced.

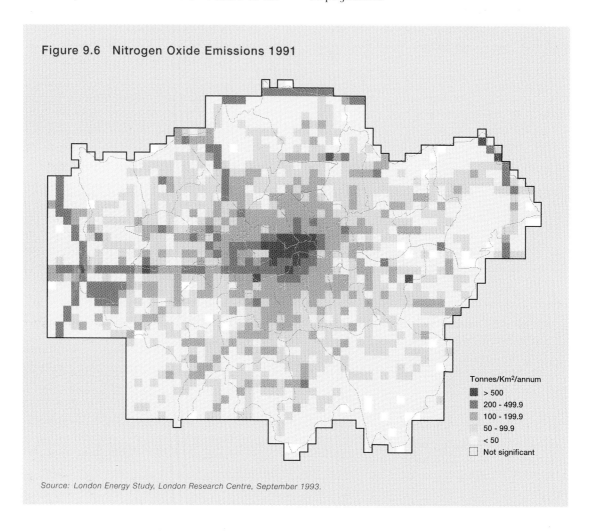

Figure 9.6   Nitrogen Oxide Emissions 1991

Tonnes/Km²/annum
- > 500
- 200 - 499.9
- 100 - 199.9
- 50 - 99.9
- < 50
- Not significant

Source: London Energy Study, London Research Centre, September 1993.

9.25.   Boroughs should:

- monitor air quality and maintain inventories of air pollutants, either individually or collectively, and formulate strategic policies to minimise pollution

- consult the relevant pollution control authorities and those responsible for environmental protection when formulating policies

- identify environmental constraints on polluting activities to ensure the protection of the air, water and land environment

- include policies to separate potentially polluting and other land uses to reduce conflicts

- set out criteria in respect of different pollutants against which plans and policies can be appraised

and proposals assessed, using local knowledge where possible

- consider the effects of transport emissions in relation to other forms of pollution, to inform traffic management and transport policies and proposals

- prepare policies for the treatment and management of contaminated land and completed landfill sites, including setting out the likely acceptability of different types of development on such sites, and the criteria to be used in assessing applications.

Noise as a source of pollution

9.26.   Large areas of London suffer relatively high levels of noise for a significant part of the day. This applies particularly to noise from road traffic, railways and aircraft. Some areas also suffer from industrial noise. All UDPs should include policies on noise, although in some cases noise control and regulation other than that under the planning system may be more appropriate. Full guidance with examples is given in PPG24 and MPG 11.

9.27. Boroughs should:

- prepare policies to ensure that noise sensitive development is sited away from significant generators of noise

- consider policies on the mix and disposition of different land uses so that noise generating development and activities take place where effects on noise sensitive development are reduced to acceptable levels relative to the characteristics of the surroundings

- set out policies either to minimise the effects of extraneous noise on noise sensitive development and sensitive areas (including recreational, important wildlife or high amenity value areas) or to limit the noise source itself.

Where it is not possible to achieve optimal locations, the imposition of planning conditions or the desirability of planning obligations should be considered to moderate adverse effects.

MINERALS

9.28. Aggregates are the main minerals to be addressed in UDPs. Local supplies in London are dwindling and there is already heavy reliance on imports. Although London supplies less than 10% of its aggregates requirements, local supplies help to ease demand elsewhere and the consequential environmental and other costs of transport and distribution. Provision should therefore be made for the extraction of potential workable resources for the foreseeable future. However, as the anticipated increase in demand will exacerbate the supply situation further it is also important to make provision for imports to London and their transport within London. Studies and on-going work by organisations such as LPAC, the South East Regional Aggregates Working Party (SERAWP) and the PLA will form a starting point for a planned approach to aggregates supply and distribution by planning authorities in London and the South East. This will be essential if a steady supply of aggregates

is to be maintained economically and in an environmentally acceptable manner. A further potentially important aggregates supply could come from greater use of demolition and construction wastes which currently comprise only about 5% of supply. There should be greater encouragement of the use of recycled materials and provision of recycling plants. Similarly, the reuse of buildings and structures rather than demolition and rebuilding may save materials.

9.29. All UDPs should address minerals issues, whether or not minerals development or activity is taking place or expected. Boroughs must be able to demonstrate that they have considered the need and realistic prospects for minerals development, transport, processing and recycling in their area. This should include encouraging:

- extraction within London where this is still feasible

- the provision of depots and wharves with space for associated activities where appropriate

- minerals recycling by establishment of demolition materials recycling plants, together with an assessment of opportunities for facilities

- efficiency in the use of aggregates

- identification of sources of raw waste materials on which the construction industry can draw.

MPG1, 2, 6 and 7 are particularly relevant.

9.30. Boroughs should include policies covering:

- where appropriate, criteria for identifying acceptable sites for mineral working (principally sand and gravel)

- identification of mineral resources for extraction as a means of contributing to the London landbank of permitted reserves of sand and gravel, at an overall level and annual production apportionment agreed by SERAWP and SERPLAN. Where this is not likely to be feasible or practicable because of limitations on workable resources, lack of planning applications or overriding environmental constraints, there should be an explanation. Potentially workable resources should be safeguarded from irreversible development which would sterilise them and, where practicable, minerals should be worked prior to such development

• environmental protection. Such policies will be particularly important in London where proposals may come forward for development in the Green Belt or MOL, near to areas of high population or other environmentally sensitive areas and where there are likely to be effects on groundwater and possibly flooding. UDPs should include criteria for site location, design and appearance, methods of working, operation and associated or ancillary activities (such as processing and batching plant and storage), including the method and scale of transport and routes. Mitigating measures to minimise unavoidable adverse effects should be addressed

• site restoration, aftercare and after-use

• a presumption in favour of the movement of aggregates by rail and water. This includes transport of aggregates (particularly hard rock) from outside the South East into London by rail; movement of sea-dredged sand and gravel, and onward movement by barge or rail of hard rock

from distant coastal superquarries landed by bulk sea-going vessels at deep water port facilities in the Thames Estuary

• criteria for the development of aggregates and demolition materials recycling facilities, including relevant environmental protection measures.

9.31. Boroughs should address the need to safeguard existing depot, wharf and associated facilities and those with potential for future use (Fig 9.7). Subject to prevailing environmental constraints, the modernisation and expansion of such facilities should be encouraged, particularly if this results in environmental improvements. Where there is an identified potential need to increase depot and wharf capacity in various parts of London, both to meet local need for aggregates and secure a balanced distribution pattern for London as a whole, Boroughs (or groups of Boroughs) should investigate opportunities for such facilities in their areas and identify potential sites. If there is no scope for such development, the UDP must explain why. Plans should include criteria which are to be applied having regard to the particular characteristics and needs of the aggregates industry in the assessment

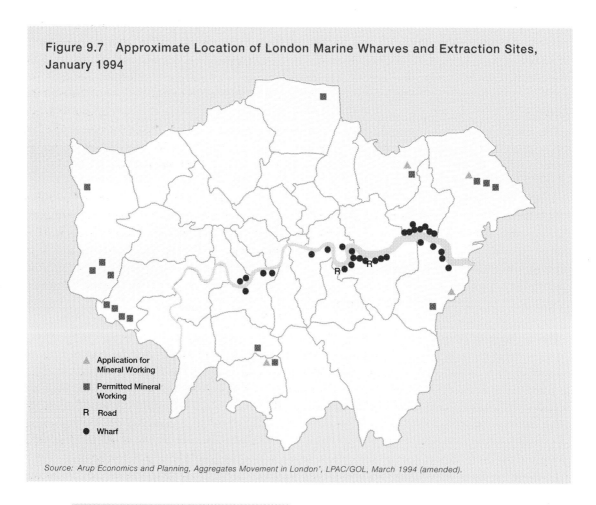

Figure 9.7   Approximate Location of London Marine Wharves and Extraction Sites, January 1994

△ Application for Mineral Working

▩ Permitted Mineral Working

R   Road

●   Wharf

Source: Arup Economics and Planning, Aggregates Movement in London', LPAC/GOL, March 1994 (amended).

of planning applications for such development, whether or not sites have been identified.

9.32. Recent and on-going studies into aggregates movement in London indicate that there may be a need for additional rail depots in certain areas of London. There are also indications that there may be a need for additional wharf capacity (which might be provided at currently non-operational wharves) to handle marine aggregates and aggregates landed in the lower Thames from, for example, coastal superquarries, then trans-shipped by barge upstream to wharves from which there would be onward movement by road or rail (LPAC 1994h, Port of London Authority 1995). The Thames Gateway Planning Framework provides guidance on the need to identify landing and transfer sites, as well as broad areas of search for new wharves. Further guidance will be included in Strategic Planning Guidance for the Thames.

WATER AND SEWERAGE

9.33. The supply of water and the disposal of waste is essential to any human settlement. Plans will need to ensure that development is planned so as not to run ahead of the necessary provision of water supply and sewerage infrastructure. This should be done in consultation with the water and sewerage undertakers and the EA. In formulating UDP policies, Boroughs should have regard to the published guidance, in particular the NRA's *Guidance Notes for Local Planning Authorities in the Methods of Protecting the Water Environment through Development Plans.* (National Rivers Authority 1994). Further Guidance on water issues is given in Chapters 2 and 7.

9.34. Notwithstanding the protection offered by the Thames Barrage, flooding could occur if a tidal surge in the estuary resulting in barrage closure coincided with a peak load of water moving down river. Low lying areas away from the Thames may also suffer flooding from other water courses at times of exceptionally high run-off. In areas prone to flooding or of potential flood risk, including that arising from increased run-off as a result of new development, Boroughs should address potential problems in UDPs if the development of land could be affected. Appropriate control policies and protection measures should be included. Circular 30/92 gives further guidance (Department of the Environment 1992).

9.35. The potential effects of development upon groundwater flows, levels and quality should be addressed. In central London, the lower Lee Valley and parts of south east London, levels of groundwater have been depressed by historic abstractions. Abstractions have now ceased and levels are rising again. Specific account will need to be taken of the effects of this on proposals for any underground construction of foundations which may penetrate into the zone into which groundwater is expected to return. There would be benefits if abstracting industries were introduced on suitable sites, to avoid the costs of pumping and other mitigating measures.

POTENTIALLY UNSTABLE LAND

9.36. Ground conditions in London are generally stable and the problems that exist from, for example, expansion and shrinkage of London clay, can be addressed through available construction technology. However, parts of London suffer from land instability problems resulting from natural geological occurrences or mining and related activity. Subsidence associated with chalk mining has occurred in several south east Boroughs; mining has also taken place in parts of south and north west London. Natural cavities in chalk, some subsequently naturally infilled, may also give rise to subsidence.

9.37. Ground problems may also arise as a result of the infilling of gravel and clay pits and quarries over several hundred years, often with refuse. Many of these are unrecorded, for example around Heathrow. Small landslips may occur naturally because of the instability of the London Clay and Claygate Beds (for example around Hampstead/Highgate and Crystal Palace) or as a result of failures of excavated slopes, for example rail and road cuttings.

9.38. Boroughs should address these issues and where possible identify potential problem areas and investigative measures prior to development. They should also set out appropriate policies to control development in affected or potentially affected areas. Further guidance is given in PPG14 and MPG12.

ENERGY

9.39. The main sources of energy currently used in significant amount in final use form in London are derived from fossil fuels and include natural gas, electricity, petrol, diesel and aviation fuel (Fig 9.8). Various other fuels and oils are used in smaller quantities. Sources originate outside London, and a significant amount of London's electricity is generated in the Midlands and the Thames Estuary

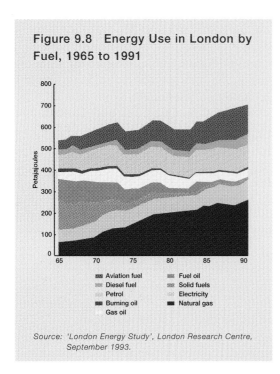

Figure 9.8 Energy Use in London by Fuel, 1965 to 1991

Aviation fuel | Fuel oil
Diesel fuel | Solid fuels
Petrol | Electricity
Burning oil | Natural gas
Gas oil

Source: 'London Energy Study', London Research Centre, September 1993.

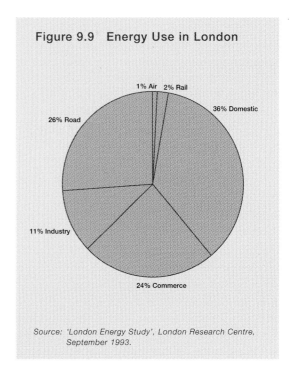

Figure 9.9 Energy Use in London

Source: 'London Energy Study', London Research Centre, September 1993.

area. Oil refining also takes place in the Thames Estuary. By far the greatest use of energy is in the domestic and commercial sectors and for cars (Fig 9.9). Other users are industry and other forms of transport. Combustion of fossil fuels is a major source of pollution and reducing their use will help reduce pollution. There is further scope for smaller electricity generation plants including gas-fired, combined heat and power, and energy from waste by incineration. Such plants help to reduce energy inputs, carbon emissions and the need for transmission lines and should be considered whenever there is substantial new development or major refurbishment of existing heating facilities. They do not need to be confined to the traditional areas of industry and sites are or may become available throughout London, making a positive contribution to sustainable development.

9.40. There may be opportunities in the future for the exploitation of renewable resources. Guidance on the role which development plans can play in securing a more sustainable approach to energy production, consumption and conservation is given in PPG12, PPG13 and PPG22. There are already opportunities for saving energy, for example through passive design principles such as securing heat gain through the design and insulation of buildings, some of which can be secured through the development control process. Boroughs should therefore include policies in UDPs:

• identifying opportunities for new or upgraded electricity generation throughout London, including combined heat and power plants, community heating schemes and generation from renewable sources. Potential sites should be identified or an explanation included as to why it is considered there are no suitable sites. Whether or not sites are identified, UDPs should set out criteria against which proposals for such facilities would be assessed

• setting out general aspects of design, orientation, density and location of buildings to maximise energy conservation and sustainability. More detailed guidance, including for example construction techniques and materials, should not be included as policies in UDPs but should be in Supplementary Planning Guidance

• to encourage specific improvements in energy efficiency for new developments and refurbishment schemes, using advice and guidance from the Department of the Environment's *Energy Efficiency Best Practice Programme* (Department of the Environment 1994e) and the Department of Trade and Industry *Energy Design Advice Scheme* (Department of Trade and Industry 1992).

• for travel patterns and modes, with emphasis on reduction of the need to travel and travel by energy efficient modes.

10.1. Continued monitoring of land use change and the needs of London's economy is essential so that UDPs can set out relevant and up to date policies. Following the adoption of the first UDP each Borough should carefully review its plan in the light of this Guidance and of the most recent national planning policy guidance. Each Borough should then decide on the scale of alterations which are necessary to adopted policies and proposals and consider its timetable for either the alteration or replacement of the plan.

10.2. This Strategic Guidance will be kept under review to provide the strategic planning framework for London, and Supplementary Guidance will be prepared when necessary. The Secretary of State requests that LPAC continue to monitor or report on the main issues considered by the London Boroughs in the implementation and review of UDPs. LPAC should ensure that strategic concerns are brought to the attention of Boroughs so that there can be an improvement in the quality of the Part Is of UDPs. The main monitoring concerns for Boroughs include:

- analysis of the characteristics, disadvantages and development potential within their areas, including local needs and opportunities

- rates of re-use of land, particularly the re-use of previously derelict sites

- continued reviews of safeguarded land to ensure that the most appropriate uses are safeguarded according to demand, especially for the industrial, financial and retail sectors and for transport

- the supply of new dwellings, adaptations, conversions and affordable housing

- the effect of new and proposed retail developments and indicators of the viability and vitality of town centres

- an assessment of transport infrastructure, including the provision of public transport, parking standards, traffic congestion and the possible transport impact of major development proposals

- the provision and quality of Green Belt land,

Metropolitan Open Land and other open spaces, including the contribution of green corridors and the River Thames to the quality of the built and natural environment

- assessment of the quality of the visual environment, including indicators on sites of special quality or character

- standards of air quality, the demand for aggregates and minerals, and levels of waste generation and disposal, including the re-use and recycling of materials and waste.

10.3. In addition, LPAC should monitor:

- Cross-Borough issues, particularly those relating to the Central Area

- the opportunities and disadvantages affecting areas within the capital, including changes in employment patterns, the nature and extent of unemployment and wider labour market issues

- density standards, particularly those relating to employment and residential uses

- London's office market, examining the different sectors of the capital's office market and changes in supply and demand

- business and industrial activity, including the availability of suitable land and the identification of sites of major development potential

- housing supply and capacity and the affects of population and household projections

- town centres' strengths and major changes in floorspace and catchments

- the development of the capital's transport system and parking provision

- consistency in the consideration of Green Belt and Metropolitan Open Land issues

- demand for aggregates and minerals and facilities for the disposal and management of waste.

10.4. Monitoring should be undertaken in the light of the objectives set out in Chapter 1 of this Guidance. Possible conflict may occur in the implementation of these objectives. Where such circumstances arise, Boroughs are expected to ensure that their decisions are based upon a clear and thorough consideration of the issues involved having regard to the context of the decision in respect of location and planning policy as set out in national Planning Policy Guidance, this Guidance and the adopted plan. This will help to insure that plans are implemented to ensure development which is both economically and environmentally sustainable.

10.5. PPG12 sets out the requirement for authorities to have regard to environmental considerations in preparing policies and general proposals in UDPs. The reviews of UDPs should include a clear account of the environmental appraisal of policies and proposals. LPAC's *State of the Environment Report for London* (LPAC 1995c) provides a starting point for this appraisal in London. This and other sources are described in the box. It will be important to strike a balance between indicators of local environmental effects and those of strategic interest. The former will be of particular value in discussions in local Agenda 21. Such discussions are likely to take place independently of development plan preparation but the results should be fed back as appropriate for consideration in the review of UDPs.

Local Agenda 21 - Key Features

Sustainability covers more than conserving natural resources and preserving the natural environment; it includes halting and preventing environmental degradation and improving existing environmental quality, embracing socio-economic as well as land use planning policy. The key features of Local Agenda 21 are:

- it provides a framework (as opposed to prescription) for sustainable development to produce a Local Agenda 21 plan at the Borough level
- it involves partnerships, consensus, and shared aims and goals, and requires consultation with local people and organisations to make sure the LA 21 plan is supported
- it requires cross-discipline, cross-interest group and cross-boundary coordination (eg waste disposal, transport)

The Association of London Government (ALG) is coordinating work across London to develop a Local Agenda 21 for London, involving stakeholders meetings and a consultative conference leading to a plan.

Environmental Appraisal

Boroughs are required to carry out an environmental appraisal of UDP policies and proposals (PPG12 para. 6.24-6.25).

The DoE *Environmental Appraisal of Development Plans: A Good Practice Guide* (Department of the Environment 1993) introduces the value and purpose of environmental appraisal and suggests a general approach for authorities to take when appraising plans. This identifies environmental impact criteria under the three general headings of global sustainability, natural resources and environmental quality. It then suggests a matrix approach in order to assess the impact of policies and proposals on the environmental impact criteria.

LPAC's *State of the Environment Report for London* (LPAC 1995c) builds on the DoE report's three environmental impact criteria. Indicators are developed for each criteria and provide a framework for monitoring the elements which affect sustainable development. The data contained in the report will need to be regularly updated to assist boroughs in meeting the requirement of PPG12 for the environmental appraisal of UDPs. The criteria selected, together with the information about them provided by the data on the indicators, provide a useful starting point. Any appraisal will need to take account of both London-wide strategic concerns as well as the local context.

Boroughs will also find it helpful to have regard to the work SERPLAN is undertaking to develop a set of sustainability principles and which will assist the environmental appraisal of UDP policies and proposals. They will need to develop their own approach to appraisal consistent with the above and incorporate it into any review of the plan. This should help achieve sustainable development and quality objectives, as well as reflect local Agenda 21 concerns in the UDP.

10.6. The London Development Monitoring System (LDMS) has proved useful in presenting a comprehensive view of large developments since the preparation of the first Strategic Guidance. It is important that it is maintained and all Boroughs must provide the London Research Centre with the necessary up to date information to maintain it as an authoritative, unique and London wide source.

Given the increasingly complex structural dimension of London, the LDMS will prove to be a major monitoring asset through its ability to provide development trend information tailored to distinct spatial areas. The Secretary of State commends it as a record of development activity and hopes that it will prove increasingly valuable in the understanding of the major land use changes in London.

London Development Monitoring System

The London Development Monitoring System (LDMS) monitors major planning development across London. ("Major" is defined as 1000 m^2 or more gross floorspace of the main commercial land uses; residential developments of 10 dwellings or more, or hotel/hostel developments of 10 bedspaces or more.

Developed by the London Research Centre in response to Secretary of State's request in 1989 Strategic Planning guidance (RPG3) for a system to monitor development within London, LDMS is supported by the Government Office for London, the Corporation of London, the London Boroughs and the London Planning Advisory Committee.

LDMS monitors individual planning decisions, building starts and completions for major developments in each principal land use class. The system is regularly updated and produces information published in annual and quarterly reports. One-off interrogations of the system can also be undertaken to provide information at sector and Borough level and down to individual sites for specific use classes.

Appendix 1

THE ROLE AND SCOPE OF GUIDANCE

1. Part II Chapter 1 of the Town and Country Planning Act, 1990 requires that each London Borough shall prepare a Unitary Development Plan (UDP) for its area. PPG12 and the Town and Country Planning (Development Plan) Regulations 1991 explain the procedures to be followed. The Regulations provide for Part I of each UDP, outlining general development and land-use policies, to reflect the Secretary of State's Strategic Guidance. The London Docklands Development Corporation should likewise have regard to this Guidance in exercising its planning and related functions.

2. The Secretary of State and his Inspectors will have regard to this Guidance in dealing with planning applications and appeals. As a material consideration in planning matters, strategic guidance has a similar status to other national and regional planning guidance set out in Circulars, in RPGs and in PPGs.

3. In 1991, Parliament strengthened the role of the development plan by amending the 1990 Act (in the Planning and Compensation Act 1991) to insert Section 54A. This Section provides that, where an authority is required to have regard to the development plan, decisions are to be in accordance with the plan unless material considerations indicate otherwise. The development plan therefore is the main component in the plan led system.

4. When reviewing their development plans local authorities should consider whether the proposed policies are consistent with national policy or regional and strategic guidance. This RPG contains certain policy advice which is specific to London and takes account of the special circumstances of the region. It may therefore vary in detail from national policy as expressed in PPGs.

5. Authorities preparing UDPs and Inspectors considering either objections to a plan at Inquiry or appeals will be expected to base their policies and decisions on the guidance set out in this RPG. Where local authorities intend to promote policies which appear to be in conflict with national or regional guidance they will be expected to give adequate reasoned justification based on the relevant specific local circumstances to warrant acceptance of such policies. The Secretary of State will consider such justification before deciding whether a formal objection or further intervention should be made.

6. The 1990 Act (as amended) states that Part I of development plans should include general policies for the use and development of land (including measures for the improvement of the physical environment, the management of traffic and the conservation of the natural beauty and amenity of the land). It is therefore important that reviews of plans consider economic development, transport and environmental improvement.

7. The Secretary of State expects Boroughs to work cooperatively on the strategic matters set out in this guidance and to prepare appropriate strategic policy in Part I of the reviewed plans. Part II of development plans should include more detailed policies for the development and use of land in their area. UDPs should therefore express policies and proposals in a way which assists development control. Policies should not be reviewed in isolation, and discussion of related matters may be included in the reasoned justification to those policies where it is relevant to a full understanding of the policies or provides a context for them.

8. Well prepared development plans that are practical and realistic can assist developers and public service organisations in considering future investment and the allocation of resources. The process of plan preparation and review enables members of the public, business and industry, and local voluntary groups to participate in decisions affecting the future of their areas. The Secretary of State hopes that they will take full advantage of the opportunities for participation that this process affords.

Appendix 2

DEVELOPMENT CONTROL POLICY FOR TRUNK ROADS IN LONDON

Introduction

1. This Appendix describes how the Highways Agency of the Department of Transport deals with development matters in the context of trunk roads in London for which it is responsible.

Policy context

2. Chapter 6 describes the constraints which apply to the capacity of the trunk road network in London and the scope for increasing capacity which is limited to improvements in orbital movement and access to areas earmarked for regeneration. In general forecasts of traffic growth in London are lower than national forecasts because of these network constraints.

3. This view of traffic growth is relevant to the policy framework within which Boroughs are encouraged to work, preparing UDPs which promote greater accessibility to and use of public transport, through the location of development where public transport accessibility is high, and which promote non-polluting modes, such as walking and cycling, through planning for mixed use developments which require less overall travel and less car dependency. These plans are to be complemented by appropriate parking restraint policies, through on street parking controls, and by restrictions on parking at new developments. By developing coherent strategies for reducing the amount of traffic generated by new development, Boroughs can seek to ensure that both the environmental impact of such development and the impact on the strategic trunk road network are minimised.

4. In this way the local planning authorities' approach to development issues can complement the Department of Transport's approach to the management and improvement of the trunk road network. The Government's objectives for the strategic tier of the hierarchy in London are set out in Chapter 6. Trunk roads and motorways form the greater part of the strategic road network in London.

The Department aims as far as possible to preserve the ability of the trunk road network to serve longer distance traffic, taking traffic away from unsuitable roads and residential areas. The Department therefore needs to consider carefully the impact of new developments on the trunk road network, bearing in mind its overall objectives and the role of trunk roads within their strategic tier of the London road hierarchy. The Highways Agency, in implementing this policy, aims to ensure that developments can proceed without compromising road safety or the efficient operation of the trunk road network. As a result, on the trunk road network, through traffic generally has priority over access to adjacent land uses with lower tier roads considered as the preferred means of access. Only where a trunk road is already having to perform significant lower tier frontage access functions will there normally be scope for considering significant additional access activity.

Applications the Agency should see

5. The General Development Order (GDO) requires local planning authorities to notify the Agency of applications involving new or altered accesses to motorways and to other trunk roads subject to a speed limit of more than 40 mph. It also requires notification of applications within 67 metres of the centre line (or such distance as may be directed) or proposals to improve or construct trunk roads.

6. The Agency is also interested in larger developments irrespective of the speed limit or distance from a trunk road, and the GDO requires local planning authorities to consult it where traffic generated is likely to have a material effect on the volume or nature of traffic entering or leaving the trunk road.

Traffic Impact Assessment

7. The Institution of Highways and Transportation (IHT) guidelines on Traffic Impact Assessment (TIA), which were welcomed by the Highways Agency, suggest the need for an assessment in the following cases;

- Residential developments in excess of 200 units

- Business (B1 & B2) Gross Floor Area (GFA) in excess of 5000 m^2

- Warehousing (B8) GFA in excess of 10000 m^2

- Retail GFA in excess of 1000 m^2

- 100 trips in/out combined in the peak hour

- 100 on site parking spaces

8.   At and above these levels, the Agency would expect to see a TIA, prepared in accordance with the IHT's recommendations, and would take the results of the TIA into account in deciding its approach to the proposed development. The Agency may also request a TIA on any development which might create significant impact on the trunk road network. It is in the applicant's interest to involve the Agency, at an early stage, to discuss and agree the input data. Developments with restricted parking set in Controlled Parking Zones where traffic generated will be minimal are likely to be acceptable.

Developments affecting the National Roads Programme

9.   As described above, the Department's trunk roads programme has the limited objectives of improving orbital movement, reducing congestion and accidents, and opening up access to areas earmarked for regeneration. The Highways Agency will normally direct against development which would require made orders or let contracts for a trunk road scheme in the National Road Programme to be amended. In other cases the Agency will normally impose conditions restricting the commencement of the development and any highway works required to accommodate the development's traffic until the trunk road scheme is delivered.

Developments affecting the existing Trunk Road Network

Forecast traffic

10.   In London the level of traffic forecast on a particular route will depend on a variety of factors. The combination of these interrelated factors will vary according to the location. These are;

- the level of forecast growth in economic activity

(which is expected to be higher in areas earmarked for regeneration such as east London, Docklands and the Thames Gateway)

- the Department of Transport's own plans for improving the road network and increasing capacity, which are limited as described above. These limited plans will constrain growth which might otherwise have occurred in areas where major road improvements are neither necessary or desirable. In other areas such as Docklands where capacity restrictions would hamper wider economic objectives, the DOT's plans are less limited, and therefore imply greater levels of growth

- the local authorities' own approach to traffic management and restraint, particularly through policies for on-street and off street parking and parking at new developments

- the relatively high public transport accessibility in many areas of London where demand for travel, particularly for commuting, can be met by means other than the private car.

Junction capacity

11.   In London, conditions at junctions tend to be the critical factor in determining the performance of the network. Broadly, the Agency considers conditions on the highway in London to be satisfactory when the ratio of flow to capacity (RFC), as measured by one of the recognised and appropriate traffic models mentioned in the Institution of Highways and Transportation guidance on Traffic Impact Assessments, does not exceed 90% at peak periods for critical sections. This is not a sharp dividing line: the closer the RFC approaches 90%, the stronger the need to address the problem becomes. Above this ratio, conditions deteriorate rapidly and it becomes likely the Agency will direct refusal unless satisfactory and environmentally acceptable trunk road improvements can be identified.

12.   Where there is no existing capacity problem (that is, RFC comfortably below 90%), the Agency will accept some erosion of capacity on sections of trunk road performing significant lower tier frontage access functions. However, the more capacity is reduced to a point where RFC equals 90% at peak periods the more persuasive the evidence supporting the development will need to be and the more minded the Agency will be to direct refusal.

13. Where there is an existing capacity problem (that is where RFC is close to or above 90%), the Agency will seek greater evidence that the development does not cause an unacceptable worsening of existing conditions at the critical sections of any critical junctions. Development will normally be acceptable where there is no significant worsening of existing queues and delays. Otherwise, the Agency will generally direct refusal unless a satisfactory highway improvement scheme can be devised and implemented.

14. Improvement schemes promoted under s278 of the Highways Act 1980 are normally designed to cope safely with total traffic forecast to arise 15 years after the full opening of the development. As explained above, in London traffic forecasts will differ from route to route. On trunk roads for which there is no improvement scheme in the Roads Programme, forecast 15 year growth may be low due to the physical limits on capacity and the problems, particularly environmental impact, involved in significantly improving capacity.

15. The Agency will discuss with applicants scenarios of traffic growth anticipated within the 15 year planning horizon on particular routes affected by proposed developments. If a growth forecast cannot be readily determined a range of sensitivity tests will be applied. Where, as occurs in a significant number of cases in London, traffic growth scenarios are constrained and either limited improvements or no improvements at all are proposed by the Agency, the Agency will seek a developer funded scheme which provides for the maximum levels of traffic growth consistent with those constraints and other relevant local factors.

Safety audits

16. As on its own schemes the Agency will normally require safety audits to be undertaken for developer-led schemes where a section 278 agreement is in place. For developer-led schemes where orders are necessary, a stage one safety audit will normally be required prior to the publication of the draft orders. For other schemes, a single safety audit incorporating both the stage 1 and stage 2 safety audits is carried out at detailed design stage. For small schemes there are often no distinct initial and detailed design stages, and the result of the safety audit will not usually be known until after planning consent has been granted. Therefore developers are strongly advised to provide an initial safety audit of the preliminary design to allow particular problems to be identified and resolved at an early stage.

Access

17. The Agency will generally require any new or altered access to be designed to the Agency's standards, though it will consider whether there are any exceptional circumstances, such as where the necessary land is not available, that would justify it relaxing its requirements. The Agency will have regard to: policy in *Circular Roads 4/88* against proliferation of trunk road accesses; both the current application and the possible potential use of the development site; the local accident record; and whether any similar accesses nearby are operating satisfactorily. The Agency will direct conditions at outline application stage to reflect proposed trunk road access arrangements but it will direct refusal where a developer proposes to leave the means of access as a reserved matter. Schemes designed solely to service developments through dedicated turning lanes, particularly those with signal controlled junctions, are unlikely to be acceptable where they involve the loss of scarce road space.

Appendix 3

TRAFFIC DIRECTOR FOR LONDON AND DEVELOPMENT CONTROL

Introduction

1.   This Appendix describes the involvement of the Traffic Director for London in development control matters. The Traffic Director for London has traffic management responsibilities for the Priority (Red) Routes designated by the Secretary of State for Transport under the Road Traffic Act 1991 ('red routes') and the roads designated by the Secretary of State for Transport under paragraph 5 of Schedule 5 to the Local Government Act 1985 ('designated roads').

2.   As the Department of Transport's *Circular 5/92 (Traffic Management and Parking Guidance)* (Department of Transport 1992) explains, London local authorities need to obtain the approval of the Traffic Director before exercising certain of their powers under the Highways Act 1980 and the Road Traffic Regulation Act 1984, including those to prohibit, restrict or regulate traffic or parking on any road which affects directly or indirectly the operation of red routes, designated roads, or both.

Development proposals affecting Priority (Red) Route Local Plans

3.   The Traffic Director's Network Plan sets the framework within which each London local authority is required to operate in relation to all red routes. The Traffic Director has been set the task of undertaking a comprehensive review and revision of the traffic management controls and measures on the 315-mile red route network. Proposals for red routes arising from the major review are contained within local plans, which are developed in conjunction with the relevant local authority. Copies of each Local Plan are held by the Traffic Director and the relevant local authority and are available for inspection at their offices. The implementation of the Local Plans is due to be completed so that the red route network is operational in 2000.

4.   Early contact with the Traffic Director should be made if development proposals are likely to affect the package of measures contained within Local Plans. Contact points are shown in the Traffic Director's *Circular TD1*, (available from the Traffic Director's office).

5. The Traffic Director recognises that some development proposals provide potential for substantial improvements to the operation of red routes. These improvements could also enable additional measures to be incorporated within Local Plans. Other proposals could require a reassessment of the package of controls and measures contained within a Local Plan. The Traffic Director and London local authorities have statutory procedures to follow before Local Plans can be amended and advance notice of development proposals is essential when amendment of Local Plans needs to be considered.

6.   Some London local authorities and developers are already consulting the Traffic Director informally to identify those instances where a local authority would be required to notify the Traffic Director of any possible change to a Local Plan arising from development proposals affecting a red route. Developers can prepare the papers for such notifications, but they must be submitted by the relevant London local authority. Further details on how these notifications should be prepared are contained in *Circular TD1.*

7.   The Traffic Director recognises that highway alterations are needed at some locations in relation to new development, and these may also create new highway capacity. The balance of how this is re-allocated is central to the achievement of Red Route objectives - to remove obstructive parking, to provide suitable parking and loading facilities where possible, to improve journey times for through traffic and buses, to enhance environmental quality, to improve bus reliability, to assist pedestrians and cyclists, to have regard for the needs of disabled people, but not to increase car commuting into or across central London. Major schemes need to be considered in relation to the timetable for implementation of the red route network and how they can be integrated with the package of measures contained within Local Plans.

Proposals affecting pedestrians, cyclists, and people with disabilities

8. Major redevelopment proposals may provide opportunities to create better conditions for other road users, such as pedestrians, cyclists and people with disabilities, and these improvements can complement the Traffic Director's own programme. The Traffic Director encourages local authorities to promote such improvements as they develop the Local Plans, in consultation with local interests such as cycling and pedestrian groups. He is likely to support facilities being provided on red routes to assist people with a disability. Further information on the approach that the Traffic Director is taking to improve facilities for pedestrians, cyclists, and people with disabilities is given in the Traffic Director's *Network Plan* (Traffic Director for London 1993).

Development proposals affecting designated roads

9. The Traffic Director also recognises that development proposals can affect designated roads. Local authorities and developers are again encouraged to discuss such instances with the Traffic Director at an early stage, especially where it can be foreseen that the traffic capacity or distributor function of the Designated Road could be impeded. *Circular TD1* gives further information on the procedures to be followed where it becomes necessary to notify the Traffic Director of any impact on a designated road arising from a development proposal.

Further guidance

10. In addition to the guidance given in *Circular TD1*, and the information contained in his *Network Plan* and red route Local Plans, the Traffic Director is developing further guidance to assist local planning authorities, developers and their agents on development control. The Traffic Director also issued a revised implementation timetable for the red routes in March 1995 in The *Network Plan Supplement* that is available from his office (Traffic Director for London 1995).

Contact Address

Traffic Director for London
College House,
Great Peter Street
LONDON
SW1P 3LN

Tel: 0171-222-4545
Facsimile: 0171-976-8640

Appendix 4

RELEVANT PLANNING POLICY GUIDANCE NOTES

	TITLE	PUBLISHED

Planning Policy Guidance Notes

	Index of Planning Guidance	Jun 1995
PPG1	General Policy and Principles	Mar 1992
PPG2	Green Belts	Jan 1995
PPG3	Housing	Mar 1992
PPG4	Industrial & Commercial Development & Small Firms	Nov 1992
PPG5	Simplified Planning Zones	Nov 1992
PPG6	Town Centres & Retail Developments	Jul 1993
PPG7	The Countryside & the Rural Economy	Jan 1992
PPG8	Telecommunications	Dec 1992
PPG9	Nature Conservation	Oct 1994
PPG12	Development Plans and Regional Planning Guidance	Feb 1992
PPG13	Transport	Mar 1994
PPG14	Development on Unstable Land	Apr 1990
PPG15	Planning & the Historic Environment	Sep 1994
PPG16	Archaeology & Planning	Nov 1990
PPG17	Sport & Recreation	Sep 1991
PPG18	Enforcing Planning Control	Dec 1991
PPG19	Outdoor Advertisement Control	Mar 1992
PPG20	Coastal Planning	Sep 1992
PPG21	Tourism	Nov 1992
PPG22	Renewable Energy	Feb 1993
PPG23	Planning & Pollution	Jul 1994
PPG24	Planning & Noise	Sep 1994

Regional Planning Guidance Notes

RPG3	Annex A Supplementary Guidance For London on the Protection of Strategic Views	Nov 1991
RPG9	Regional Planning Guidance for the South East	Mar 1994
RPG9A	Thames Gateway Planning Framework	Jun 1995

continued overleaf

TITLE		PUBLISHED

Minerals Planning Guidance Notes

MPG1	General consideration and the Development Plan System	Jan 1988
MPG2	Applications, Permissions and Conditions	Jan 1988
MPG3	Coal Mining and Colliery Spoil Disposal	Jul 1994
MPG4	The Review of Mineral Working Sites	Sep 1988
MPG5	Minerals Planning and the General Development Order	Dec 1988
MPG6	Guidelines for Aggregates Provision in England	Apr 1994
MPG7	The Reclamation of Mineral Workings	Sep 1989
MPG8	Planning and Compensation Act 1991: Interim Development Order Permissions (IDOs) - Statutory Provisions and Procedures	Sep 1991
MPG9	Planning and Compensation Act 1991. Interim Development Order Permissions (IDOS) - Conditions	Mar 1992
MPG10	Provision of Raw Material for the Cement Industry	1991
MPG11	Control of Noise at Surface Mineral Workings	Apr 1993
MPG12	Treatment of Disused Mine Openings and Availability of Information on Mined Ground	Mar 1994
MPG13	Guidelines for Peat Provision in England, including the place of alternative minerals	Jul 1995
MPG14	Environment Act 1995: Review of Mineral Planning Permissions	Sep 1995

Future MPGs

Silica Sand

Landslides and Planning

Stability in quarrying

Oil and Gas

Other planning guidance under preparation;

Strategic Guidance for the Thames

References

Association of London Government (1995)
Setting the Agenda for London.
London: Association of London Government.

Chartered Institute of Housing (1993)
A Guide to Local Housing Needs Assessment.
Report prepared by Valli van Zigl. Coventry:
Chartered Institute of Housing (November).

Countryside Commission (1993)
Action for London's Trees: Investing in a leafy capital.
Task Force Trees. Advisory Booklet. Ref CCP433.
Cheltenham: Countryside Commission.

Department of the Environment (1987)
The Town and Country Planning (Use Classes) Order 1987
Statutory Instrument 1987 No.764
(as amended by S.I.1991 No.1567; S.I.1992 No.610; S.I.1994 No.724). London: HMSO.

Department of the Environment (1992)
Development and Flood Risk.
DoE Circular 30/92. London: HMSO.

Department of the Environment (1993)
Environmental Appraisal of Development Plans: A good practice guide.
London: HMSO.

Department of the Environment (1994a)
Gypsy Sites and Planning.
DoE Circular 1/94. London: HMSO.

Department of the Environment (1994b)
Planning for Affordable Housing.
Study report by Policy Studies Institute, University of Sussex, Portland Planning Consultants Ltd.
London: HMSO (March).

Department of the Environment (1994c)
Vital and Viable Town Centres: Meeting the challenge.
Report by Urban & Economic Development Group (Urbed), with Comedia, Hillier Parker, Bartlett School of Planning at University College London, and Environmental & Transport Planning, for DoE. London: HMSO (May).

Department of the Environment (1994d)
Quality in Town and Country: A discussion document.
London: DoE. (July).

Department of the Environment (1994e)
Energy Efficiency Best Practice Programme.
Paper by the then Energy Efficiency Office.
London: DoE.

Department of the Environment (1995a)
1991 Deprivation Index: A review of approaches and a matrix of results.
London: HMSO.

Department of the Environment (1995b)
Index of Local Conditions: An analysis based on 1991 Census data.
London: DoE (published May 1994, revised February 1995).

Department of the Environment (1995c)
The Thames Gateway Planning Framework.
RPG9a. London: HMSO.

Department of the Environment (1995d)
Quality in Town and Country: Urban design campaign.
London: DoE. (June).

Department of the Environment (1995e)
Projections of Households in England to 2016.
Report on 1992-based projections. London: HMSO.

Department of the Environment with Department of Transport (1995)
PPG13: A Guide to Better Practice: Reducing the need to travel through land use and transport planning.
Prepared jointly with JMP Consultants Limited, Llewelyn Davies, the Bartlett School at University College London, and South Bank University.
London: HMSO.

Department of Trade and Industry (1992 onwards)
Energy Design Advice Scheme.
Information available from regional EDAS Centres. In London: Bartlett School of Graduate Studies, Torrington Place Site, University College London, Gower Street, London, WC1E 6BT. Tel 0171 916 3891.

Department of Transport (1992)
Traffic Management and Parking Guidance.
DoT Circular 5/92. London: HMSO.

Department of Transport (1993)
Runway Capacity to Serve the South East.
London: HMSO (July).

Department of Transport (1995)
London Heliport Study.
London: DoT (March).

English Heritage with LPAC (1995)
Conservation in London: A study of strategic planning policy in London.
London: English Heritage (January).

English Nature (1994)
Planning for Wildlife in Towns and Cities.
Report prepared by David Tyldesley & Associates. Peterborough: English Nature.

Government Office for London (1995a)
Thames Strategy.
Study report prepared and designed by Ove Arup Partnership. London: HMSO.

Government Office for London (1995b)
City Walks in London.
Study report by Land Use Consultants. London: Government Office for London.

Government Office for London with Countryside Commission (1995c)
Study of London's Green Corridors: Greening the open land that adjoins the main transport routes into London.
Summary and technical reports prepared by The Adams Loxton Partnership Limited, Roger Tym and Partners, Land Management Services, Sir William Halcrow & Partners Limited, and Brian G Crane & Associates. London: Government Office for London with Countryside Commission.

Government Office for London (1996a)
London in the UK Economy: A planning perspective.
Report prepared by Arup Economic & Planning, with The Greater London Group of the London School of Economics, London Research Centre, Comedia, and Professor Peter Hall. London: DoE.

Government Office for London (1996b)
London's Urban Environment: Planning for quality.
Summary report prepared by BDP Planning. London: HMSO. A detailed technical working report is also available from Government Office for London.

HM Government (1985).
Airports Policy
Command Paper 9542. London: HMSO.

HM Government (1990)
This Common Inheritance: Britain's Environmental Strategy.
Command Paper 1200. London: HMSO.

HM Government (1994a)
Sustainable Development: The UK Strategy.
Command Paper 2426. London: HMSO.

HM Government (1994b)
Competitiveness: Helping business to win.
Command Paper 2563. London: HMSO.

HM Government (1995a)
Competitiveness: Forging ahead.
Command Paper 2867. London: HMSO.

HM Government (1995b)
Our Future Homes: Opportunity, choice, responsibility.
Command Paper 2901. London: HMSO.

HM Government (1995c)
Making Waste Work: A strategy for sustainable waste management in England & Wales.
Command Paper 3040. London: HMSO.

Institution of Highways and Transportation (1994)
Guidelines for Traffic Impact Assessment.
London: Institution of Highways and Transportation (September).

London Ecology Unit (1984 onwards)
Ecology Handbooks Nos. 1 to 26, continuing.
Details available from: London Ecology Unit,
Bedford House, 125 Camden High Street,
London, NW1 7JR. Tel 0171 267 7944.

LPAC (1993)
*Landscape Change in London's Green Belt and
Metropolitan Open Land: A study of strategic
policy.*
Ref CON31 (May). Report prepared by Land Use
Consultants for LPAC and DoE. London: London
Planning Advisory Committee.

LPAC (1994a)
*Advice on Strategic Planning Guidance for
London.*
Ref ADV26 (March). London: London Planning
Advisory Committee.

LPAC (1994b)
*Prospects and Planning Requirements of the
Creative Industries in London.*
Report prepared by Urban Cultures Ltd for LPAC
and DoE. Ref CON47 (March). London: London
Planning Advisory Committee.

LPAC (1994c)
*Offices to Homes in Central London: The capacity
for change.*
Report prepared by Applied Property Research for
LPAC and DoE. Ref CON49 (March). London:
London Planning Advisory Committee.

LPAC (1994d)
London Labour Market Budgets.
Report prepared by Business Strategies Ltd for
LPAC and DoE. Ref CON48 (April). London:
London Planning Advisory Committee.

LPAC (1994e)
London's Housing Capacity.
Ref ADV25 (June). Report prepared by London
Research Centre with Ian Haywood Partnership.
London: London Planning Advisory Committee.

LPAC (1994f)
The Quality of London's Residential Environment.
Report prepared by Llewelyn-Davies, with South
Bank University and Environment Trust Associates,
for LPAC and DoE. Ref CON45 (July). London:
London Planning Advisory Committee.

LPAC (1994g)
Transport and Distribution in London.
Report prepared by Berkeley Hanover Consulting
for LPAC and DoE. Ref CON46 (July). London:
London Planning Advisory Committee.

LPAC (1994h)
Aggregates Movement in London.
Report prepared by Arup Economics and Planning
for LPAC and Government Office for London.
Ref CON40 (August). London: London Planning
Advisory Committee.

LPAC (1994i)
High Accessibility and Town Centres in London.
Report prepared by Urban & Economic
Development Group (Urbed), with Halcrow Fox
and Donaldsons, for LPAC and DoE. Ref CON41
(August). London: London Planning Advisory
Committee.

LPAC (1994j)
London's Housing Provision 1987-93.
Ref ADV34 (November). London: London
Planning Advisory Committee.

LPAC (1995a)
*Policy, Criteria and Procedures for Identifying
Nature Conservation Sites in London.*
Committee Report No. 12/95 (14 March 1995),
formally adopting consolidation and updating
document on policy, criteria and procedures by
London Ecology Unit (January 1994). London:
London Planning Advisory Committee.

LPAC (1995b)
Residential Environment and Density
Executive Sub-Committee, Report No. 27/95
(9 May 1995). London: London Planning
Advisory Committee.

LPAC (1995c)
State of the Environment Report for London.
Report prepared by LPAC, London Boroughs,
Corporation of London, Land Use Consultants,
and London Research Centre. Loose leaf format,
anticipating updating. London: London Planning
Advisory Committee (July).

LPAC (1995d)
Town Centres Network & Policy: Progress.
Executive Sub-Committee, Report No. 65/95
(7 November 1995). London: London Planning
Advisory Committee.

LPAC (1995e)
London Office Policy Review.
Report prepared by London Property Research for LPAC, Government Office for London, and Corporation of City of London. Ref CON59 (December). London: London Planning Advisory Committee.

LPAC (1995f)
Technology Parks in London.
Report prepared by Segal Quince Wicksteed Limited for LPAC and Government Office for London. Ref CON60 (December). London: London Planning Advisory Committee.

London Pride Partnership (1994)
London Pride Prospectus.
London: London Pride Partnership (December).

London Research Centre et al. (1992)
Houses into Flats: Study of private sector conversions in London.
Report prepared by London Research Centre with Health & Housing Group and John Sizer for LPAC and DoE. Volume I: Report of Main Findings. London: HMSO. Volume II available from Department of the Environment.

London Research Centre with Department of Transport (1994)
Travel in London: London Area Transport Survey 1991.
London: HMSO.

London Sport (1990)
A Playing Fields Strategy for London.
London: London Council for Sport and Recreation.

London Sport (1994)
The Sporting Capital: The Regional Recreation Strategy for London. London: London Region, Sports Council.

London Transport Planning (1995)
New Ideas for Public Transport in Outer London.
London: London Transport Planning.

LWRA (1995)
Today's Waste, Tomorrow's Resources: The Waste Management Plan for Greater London 1995-2015.
London: London Waste Regulation Authority (January).

National Rivers Authority (1994)
Guidance Notes for Local Planning Authorities on the Methods of Protecting the Water Environment through Development Plans.
Bristol: National Rivers Authority (January).

Port of London Authority (1995)
Port Development Strategy: Aggregates.
Consultation Draft. London: Port of London Authority (December).

SERPLAN (1992)
Waste: Its reduction, re-use and disposal.
Paper RPC2266.1. London: SERPLAN.

SERPLAN (1994)
Developing the Waste Planning Guidelines: Advice on planning for waste reduction, treatment and disposal in the South East 1994-2005.
Paper RPC2700. London: SERPLAN.

Sports Council (1991)
The Playing Pitch Strategy.
Central Council for Sport and Recreation, National Playing Fields Association. London: Sports Council.

Traffic Director for London, (1993)
Network Plan.
Traffic Director for London, London.
Traffic Director for London, (1995). The Network Plan Supplement. Traffic Director for London, London.

Traffic Director for London, (1995)
The Network Plan Supplement.
Traffic Director for London, London.

Glossary of abbreviations

129

ALG	Association of London Government
AQMA	Air Quality Management Area
CSO	Central Statistical Office
CTRL	Channel Tunnel Rail Link
DoT	Department of Transport
DoE	Department of the Environment
DTI	Department of Trade and Industry
ERDF	European Reconstruction and Development Fund
BPEO	Best Practicable Environmental Option
GDO	General Development Order
GOL	Government Office for London
HMIP	Her Majesty's Inspectorate of Pollution
IHT	Institute of Highways and Transportation
LDDC	London Docklands Development Corporation
LDMS	London Development Monitoring System
LPAC	London Planning Advisory Committee
LTB	London Tourist Board
LWRA	London Waste Regulation Authority
MOL	Metropolitan Open Land
NNR	National Nature Reserve
NRA	National Rivers Authority
ONS	Office of National Statistics
OPCS	Office of Population Censuses and Surveys
PLA	Port of London Authority
RFC	Ratio of Flow to Capacity
ROSE	Rest of South East (ie outside London)
RUCATSE	Runway Capacity in the South East study
SAC	Special Areas of Conservation
SERAWP	South East Region Aggregates Working Party
SERPLAN	South East Regional Planning Conference
SEWRAC	South East Waste Regulation Advisory Committee
SPA	Special Protection Area
SRB	Single Regeneration Budget
SSSI	Site of Special Scientific Interest
SWELTRAC	South West London Transport Conference
TEC	Training and Enterprise Council
TIA	Traffic Impact Assessment
UDP	Unitary Development Plan

Printed in the United Kingdom for HMSO
Dd 302720 C25 5/96 66540